Endorsements

"Some of us who fell in love with John Owen's writings did so, to some significant measure, because of the enthusiastic endorsement given by Sinclair Ferguson. For me, after more than thirty-five years of gospel ministry, it would be difficult to exaggerate the importance of Owen's theological and pastoral insights. But we have long been in need of an updated biography—not simply one that narrates the significant details of his life, but one that analyzes the contours of his theological insights and how they shaped and defined him. And no one is better placed to do that than Sinclair Ferguson. I suspect that many of us, when engaging in word-association, provide the name 'Ferguson' when 'John Owen' is mentioned.

"I cannot overstate the importance of this volume. I fully expect it to become a best-seller among those who appreciate Owen—and deservedly so."

—Dr. Derek W.H. Thomas
Senior minister, First Presbyterian Church, Columbia, S.C.
Chancellor's Professor of Systematic and Pastoral Theology
Reformed Theological Seminary

"This is now the prime book I will be recommending on John Owen. I am very impressed, but not surprised: Sinclair Ferguson has so imbibed the spirit of Owen that he conveys the thought and heart of the great man with limpid clarity. This means that this book is far more than an introduction to Owen; it is at the same time a rich and deeply affecting meditation on communion with our glorious, triune God. Here is a feast of angel's food."

—Dr. Michael Reeves
President and professor of theology
Union School of Theology, Bridgend, Wales

"Let me begin by echoing Sinclair Ferguson's own story: John Owen, more than any other theologian of the past, has profoundly shaped my vision of the triune God and what it means to live in the wonder of the gospel. In this delightful little book, Ferguson offers a sort of expert paraphrase and appreciation of Owen's classic volume *Communion with God*. Along the way, he gives us a great gift: in your hands is now a beautifully accessible tour of Owen's approach to the spiritual life, by which he means a life secure in the love of the Father, the grace of the Son, and the strong fellowship of the Spirit. Read, savor, and be refreshed, for neither Owen nor Ferguson will disappoint."

—DR. KELLY M. KAPIC
Professor of theological studies
Covenant College, Lookout Mountain, Ga.

"Reading this book is like listening in on a conversation between one of the most trusted voices from the past and one of the most trusted voices in the present. In fact, that's exactly what this book is. And as you listen in, you will hear the arc of the conversation bend in one constant direction. You will hear these two voices remind you of the glorious truth that the Christian life is communion with the Triune God."

—DR. STEPHEN J. NICHOLS
President, Reformation Bible College, Sanford, Fla.
Chief academic officer, Ligonier Ministries

A Long Line of Godly Men Profile

The Trinitarian Devotion *of*

John Owen

SINCLAIR B. FERGUSON

ℝ *Reformation Trust* A DIVISION OF LIGONIER MINISTRIES, ORLANDO, FL

The Trinitarian Devotion of John Owen
© 2014 by Sinclair B. Ferguson

Published by Reformation Trust Publishing
a division of Ligonier Ministries
421 Ligonier Court, Sanford, FL 32771
Ligonier.org   ReformationTrust.com

Printed in Crawfordsville, Indiana
LSC Communications
0000320
First edition, third printing

ISBN 978-1-56769-403-1 (Hardcover)
ISBN 978-1-56769-430-7 (ePub)
ISBN 978-1-56769-431-4 (Kindle)

Cover illustration: Steven Noble
Interior design and typeset: Katherine Lloyd, The DESK

All Scripture quotations are from the ESV® Bible (The Holy Bible,
English Standard Version®), copyright © 2001 by Crossway, a
publishing ministry of Good News Publishers. Used by permission. All
rights reserved.

Library of Congress Cataloging-in-Publication Data

Ferguson, Sinclair B.
The Trinitarian devotion of John Owen / Sinclair B. Ferguson.
  pages cm. -- (A long line of godly men profile)
  Includes bibliographical references and index.
  ISBN 978-1-56769-403-1 -- ISBN 1-56769-403-9
1. Trinity--History of doctrines. 2. Owen, John, 1616-1683. 3. Church
history--17th century. I. Title.
BT109.F47 2014
231'.044--dc23   2014017012

To
Alistair Begg

ὁ ἀγαπητὸς ἀδελφὸς
καὶ πιστὸς διάκονος
καὶ σύνδουλος ἐν κυρίῳ

—Colossians 4:7

TABLE OF CONTENTS

Followers Worthy to be Followed

Down through the centuries, God has raised up a long line of godly men whom He has mightily used at strategic moments in church history. These valiant individuals have come from all walks of life, from the ivy-covered halls of elite schools to the dusty back rooms of tradesmen's shops. They have arisen from all points of this world, from highly visible venues in densely populated cities to obscure hamlets in remote places. Yet despite these differences, these pivotal figures have had much in common.

Each man possessed an unwavering faith in the Lord Jesus Christ, but more than that, each of these stalwarts of the faith held deep convictions in the God-exalting truths known as the doctrines of grace. Though they differed in secondary matters of theology, they nevertheless stood shoulder to shoulder in championing these biblical teachings that magnify the sovereign grace of God in salvation. These spiritual leaders upheld the foundational truth that "salvation is of the Lord."[1]

Any survey of church history reveals that those who have embraced these Reformed truths have been granted extraordinary confidence in their God. Far from paralyzing these spiritual giants, the doctrines of grace kindled within their hearts a reverential awe for God that humbled their souls before His throne. The truths of divine sovereignty emboldened these men to rise up and advance the cause of Christ on the earth. With an enlarged vision for the expansion of His kingdom upon the earth, they stepped forward boldly to accomplish the work of ten, even twenty men. They arose with wings like eagles and soared over their times. The doctrines of grace empowered them to serve God in their divinely appointed hour of history, leaving a godly inheritance for future generations.

This Long Line of Godly Men Profiles series highlights key figures in the agelong procession of these sovereign-grace men. The purpose of this series is to explore how these figures used their God-given gifts and abilities to impact their times and further the kingdom of heaven. Because they were wholly devoted followers of Christ, their examples are worthy of emulation today.

This volume, written by my good friend Sinclair Ferguson, focuses upon the man regarded as the greatest of the English Puritan theologians, John Owen. The monumental

---

1   Ps. 3:8; Jonah 2:9.

life of Owen was marked by his superior intellectual achievement. He became a pastor, chaplain to Oliver Cromwell, and vice-chancellor of the University of Oxford. His most influential work, *The Death of Death in the Death of Christ* (1647), written when Owen was only thirty-one years old, is an extended reflection on the intra-Trinitarian life of God in the incarnation and atonement of Jesus Christ. This seminal volume launched Owen on a path of Trinitarian meditation and reflection. He left behind rich treatises and sermons on the Trinitarian communion that a Christian can enjoy with the Father, Son, and Holy Spirit. Perhaps no other English theologian has spent more time in contemplation of the eternal Godhead, and Owen's study translated into a zealous passion for the gospel and devotion to Christ. John Owen stands as a towering figure, eminently worthy to be profiled in this series.

May the Lord use this book to raise up a new generation of believers who will bring the gospel message to bear upon this world. Through this profile, may you be strengthened to walk in a manner worthy of your calling. May you be zealous in your devotion to the Father, Son, and Holy Spirit, for the glory of His name and advance of His kingdom.

Soli Deo gloria!
—Steven J. Lawson
Series editor

The Christian's Greatest Privilege

I am grateful to my friend Steve Lawson for his invitation to contribute to the Long Line of Godly Men Profiles series, which he both devised and continues to edit. *Invitation* is probably too weak a word to describe his desire that this excellent series contain a volume on John Owen. I suspect he knew that, for me, writing on Owen would be something of a personal experience. For his insistence, encouragement, and friendship, I am deeply grateful. Writing *The Trinitarian Devotion of John Owen* has turned me back once more to reflect on the life and ministry of a truly great and godly man, one to whom I owe a huge personal debt.

John Owen lived from 1616 to 1683. Many of his works were published during his lifetime and a number were published soon thereafter. Two different collections of his writings appeared in the nineteenth century. But by the middle of the twentieth century, both his name and his books had fallen into virtual obscurity.

In the providence of God, Owen's *Works* began to be republished in 1965.[1] At that time, I had just turned seventeen and was in my first year at university. My tuition fees, all living expenses, and more were covered by scholarships and—happy days—there was even money left over to buy books. Slightly damaged copies of the massive volumes of Owen's *Works* (they average around six hundred pages each) could be purchased for the equivalent of a dollar or so each. I bought them one by one, sometimes two by two, until I owned a complete set.

And I began to read.

Owen's style is usually regarded as notoriously difficult. Latin was virtually his first language. His education was in Latin; he lectured in Latin; he wrote in Latin. He probably dreamed in Latin. Not surprisingly, his English style is heavily Latinate.

Yet, as I have been writing this book, it has dawned on me that God's providence had already prepared me to keep reading. As I stood on the verge of a university education, I felt very unsure of what to expect, or whether a degree was even within my intellectual power to attain. No one in my family line, as far as I knew, had ever gone to university. In those days, places were scarce. For my parents, who had both left school in their

---

1. The Banner of Truth Trust republished Owen's *The Death of Death in the Death of Christ* in 1959 and then from 1965 to 1968 reprinted the 1850–53 edition of his complete works edited by W.H. Goold, with the exception of his Latin writings. In 1991, the Trust then reprinted Owen's massive commentary on Hebrews, which had been published in the Goold edition in 1854–55.

very early teens, university studies would have been beyond their wildest aspirations. But they were deeply committed to encouraging their sons to understand the importance of education. There was no discussion, as far as I can remember, about whether we would study Latin. It was a key to further education, and therefore nonnegotiable. Little could my father and mother have imagined that the guidance they gave their eleven-year-old son would make it much easier for him, some six years later, to read the greatest, if possibly the most difficult, of all the seventeenth-century English theologians.

And so I kept reading. Of course, some of Owen's works were of greater interest to me than others. But then, some of them contained material that had probably first been preached to college students my own age. Owen stretched my mind, analyzed my soul, taught me theological devotion, and prescribed spiritual medicine. Theologically and pastorally, he helped shape what I thought a minister of the gospel should know, believe, and preach. He showed me how to think through the gospel and its application.

Owen's assistant, David Clarkson (no mean theologian himself), said in his funeral sermon, "I need not tell you of this who knew him, that it was his great design to promote holiness in the life and exercise of it among you."[2] Just as Owen's writings had done that for others, so they did it for me, encouraging me to think and live for the glory of God.

---

2. *The Works of John Owen*, ed. Thomas Russell, 21 vols. (London: Robert Baynes, 1826), 1:420.

Thus, this seventeenth-century Oxford academic and minister has been one of the most significant influences on my life. I am profoundly grateful for him—and for the way he used his gifts for the church of Christ in the stressful days in which he lived. He surely never could have dreamed that, three centuries after his death, his work would nourish a teenage boy who hoped to follow his example and become a minister of the gospel of Jesus Christ.

So—although it may not be immediately apparent to readers of the pages that follow—Dr. Lawson was right in thinking that this little book would mean something quite personal to me. For it gives me the privilege of introducing Owen to some who may never have heard his name, much less read his works. In particular, it provides an opportunity to say something about the enormous importance and relevance of a central theme in his theology. This theme can, I think, be summed up in the following way.

There is nothing in all the world more important to you than these truths:

(1) God is Trinity: Father, Son, and Holy Spirit. This is a great mystery—because we are not God and we cannot fully understand the sheer, wonderful, glorious mystery of His being. But we can begin to grasp it, and learn to love and adore Him.

(2) If you are a Christian, it is because of the loving thought and action of each person of the Trinity. The Father, along

with the Son and the Spirit, planned it before the foundation of the world; the Son came to pay the price for your redemption and, supported by the Holy Spirit, became obedient to His Father in your place, both in His life and death, to bring you justification before God; and now, by the powerful work of the Holy Spirit sent by both the Father and the Son, you have been brought to faith.

(3) The greatest privilege any of us can have is this: we can know God as Father, Son, and Holy Spirit. We can enjoy fellowship—what Owen calls "communion"—with God. This knowledge is as rich, wide, deep, long, and high as are the three persons of God. Knowing Him and having fellowship with Him is an entire world of endless knowledge, trust, love, joy, fellowship, pleasure, and satisfaction.

This is what John Owen wanted Christians to know.

The Trinitarian Devotion of John Owen is only a beginning point in explaining what all this means. But I hope it will be a beginning without an ending.

Every author is a debtor. In addition to my debt to Steve Lawson for his invitation, I am grateful to the wonderful staff of Ligonier Ministries and Reformation Trust for their encouragement and support. In a special way, I want to express my thanks to my wife, Dorothy. We met the same year I first met *The Works of John Owen*. Wherever we have gone, Owen has come with us. I have often seen in her what Owen taught about the Christian's "returns" to the Father, the Son, and the Holy Spirit in a life lived in practical devotion to Him. It is from within this context of her faithfulness to me and her love for our family that these pages come. I pray that they might stimulate in you a richer experience of the Trinitarian devotion that John Owen both tasted and taught.

—Sinclair B. Ferguson
Carnoustie, Scotland
March 2014

CHAPTER ONE

Pastor
and Theologian

A pastor, a scholar, a divine of the first magnitude; holiness gave a divine luster to his other accomplishments, it shined in his whole course, and was diffused through his whole conversation.[1]

—DAVID CLARKSON,
FUNERAL SERMON FOR JOHN OWEN,
SEPTEMBER 4, 1683

The year of his birth—1616—was the year of William Shakespeare's death.

When he was only thirty-three years old, he preached before the English Parliament. It was not for the first time, but on this occasion, King Charles I had been publicly executed less than twenty-four hours before.

At the age of thirty-six, he was appointed to be vice-chancellor

---

1. Peter Toon, *God's Statesman: The Life and Work of John Owen* (Exeter, England: Paternoster Press, 1971), p. 173.

of the University of Oxford (in American terms, the president) by the English general and future Lord Protector Oliver Cromwell.

In 1662, along with around two thousand other ministers, he was ejected from the Church of England for refusing to conform to the use of the Book of Common Prayer in church services.

Thereafter, under the threat of arrest, he served as the pastor of Nonconformist congregations. During the last period of his life, he pastored a congregation in London.

He died in 1683, leaving behind him a legacy of writings that now occupy twenty-four large volumes averaging around six hundred pages each.

His name was John Owen. In his own time, he was England's greatest living theologian. Now, more than three hundred years after his death, many still regard him as such. But who was he?

EARLY LIFE

John Owen was born in Stadham (now Stadhampton), about ten miles southeast of Oxford. His father, Henry, was the minister of the local congregation.[2] He had an older brother, William (who also became a minister[3]), and two younger brothers, Henry (who entered the military) and Philemon

---

2. Owen Sr. later became minister at Harpsden, and he died there on September 18, 1649. He is buried in the chancel of the church.

3. William was minister in Ewelme in Oxfordshire and died in 1660 at age forty-eight.

(who was killed while on military duty in Ireland in 1649), and a sister whose name is unknown.[4]

The Owens were a Puritan family. "I was bred up from my infancy under the care of my father," Owen wrote, "who was a Nonconformist all his days, and a painful [hard-working] labourer in the vineyard of the Lord."[5]

Scholars have long debated what constitutes a "Puritan." The term describes a wide variety of individuals, ranging from Anglicans who simply wanted to see the Church of England purified from some of its unbiblical features to individuals who, in their opposition to the Church of England, stood on the margins of Christian orthodoxy. Henry Owen, as his son John would later do, stood in the mainstream of biblical orthodoxy and was perhaps concerned only to see biblical guidelines followed in the worship and governance of the church. In any event, he was a faithful gospel minister and father. As Calvin said of Timothy, so we could say of Owen: he "sucked in godliness with his mother's milk."[6]

Having received his early education from his father, when he was around ten years old, thanks to a generous uncle, both he and his elder brother, William, were sent to a small school

---

4. She married John Hartcliffe, minister of Harding in Oxfordshire and later canon of Windsor. He died in 1702.

5. *The Works of John Owen*, ed. W.H. Goold, 24 vols. (Edinburgh, Scotland: 1850–53; repr. London: Banner of Truth Trust, 1966), 13:224. Subsequent citations of Owen's *Works* refer to this edition.

6. John Calvin, *Commentary on 2 Corinthians, 1 and 2 Timothy, Titus, Philemon*, ed. D.W. and T.F. Torrance, trans. T.A. Smail (Edinburgh, Scotland: Oliver and Boyd, 1964), p. 292.

in Oxford to prepare for entry to Queen's College in Oxford University.

Students at Oxford in the seventeenth century were by and large either gentlemen or scholars, but rarely both. In many ways, the university served as a kind of educational finishing school for the upper classes, many of whom would neither take exams nor graduate. Owen, however, entered the university with a view to study, and he graduated with a bachelor of arts alongside his brother in 1632, at age fifteen or sixteen. In essence, the bachelor's degree was merely preparatory to the master's degree studies that followed. He duly graduated with a master of arts in 1635.

Owen's education was classical: logic, philosophy, mathematics, ancient history, astronomy, Greek, and Hebrew. Latin was the *lingua franca* of the academic world (from college sermons to lectures and debates). Against that background, it is perhaps not surprising that Owen had as much facility in Latin as in English—indeed, perhaps more, since much of his written English scarcely masks its deep Latin influences.

Clearly, Owen benefited enormously from his studies. He had an outstandingly able academic tutor in Thomas Barlow.[7] And he did not neglect the Latin maxim *mens sana in corpore*

---

7. Carl Trueman has underscored various ways in which Owen's education and thinking may have been directly influenced by Barlow (1607–91), who, although he conformed and became bishop of Lincoln, remained a lifelong friend of Owen. See Carl R. Trueman, *John Owen: Reformed Catholic, Renaissance Man* (Farnham, Surrey, England: Ashgate, 2007), especially chapter 2.

sano (a healthy mind in a healthy body[8]). He ran, threw javelin, and enjoyed playing the flute (he later appointed his teacher Thomas Wilson to the chair of music in the university). Clearly, he was a serious student, and he disciplined himself to the extent that he often took only four hours of sleep.[9]

On graduation, Owen's intention was to engage in the prolonged studies required to attain the bachelor of divinity degree (then a seven-year program). But Oxford University had fallen under influences alien to Owen's Puritan background. William Laud had been appointed university chancellor in 1630 en route to becoming archbishop of Canterbury some three years later. King Charles I had already forbidden debates on the Calvinistic themes of election and predestination, and Laud followed this through with the catholicizing of the ethos of college life and the reintroduction of high liturgy in chapel worship, all mingled with Arminian theology.

The signs did not look auspicious for a Puritan student in divinity, and after a further two years of study, Owen left to become family chaplain and tutor in the home of Sir Robert Dormer in Ascot, shortly thereafter accepting a similar position in the house of Lord Lovelace at Hurley. Here, presumably, his duties were not onerous, and he had leisure to continue his studies. Lord Lovelace, however, was a supporter

---

8. The expression appears to have been first used by the Roman satirist Juvenal, *Satires,* 10.356.

9. Like others before and since, when in ill health in later life, Owen regretted the punishment he had given his physical resources as a younger man.

of the king in the building conflict with Parliament, and in 1642, Owen moved on to take up residence in London.

NEW BEGINNINGS

The year Owen arrived in London, the English Civil War broke out.[10] Now in the capital, Owen was able to follow the crucial events of the day firsthand. More important, however, was a more personal experience that was to change his life permanently.

By all accounts, Owen developed into a warm and genial individual. But he rarely gives himself away in his writings. If he kept journals, as many Puritans did, they were presumably destroyed at the time of his death. But what seems clear at this stage in his life—he was then in his mid-twenties—is that while he was committed to Puritan principles, he had no settled assurance that he belonged to Christ. On occasion in his published works, he gives scarcely veiled hints that he experienced deep spiritual distress.

One Sunday in 1642, he went with his cousin to hear the celebrated Presbyterian minister Edmund Calamy preach at St. Mary's, Aldermanbury. But Calamy was unable to preach, and his substitute was a little-known minister. Despite his

---

10. The First and Second Civil Wars (1642–45 and 1648–49) were part of a prolonged conflict between the English Parliament and Charles I, and came to a climax with the execution of Charles on January 30, 1649. A Third Civil War (1649–51) saw the replacement of the monarchy by a Commonwealth (1649–53) and from 1653–59 by the Protectorate of Oliver Cromwell. On the failure of Cromwell's son Richard, the monarchy was restored by the English Parliament in 1660.

cousin's prompting, Owen had no heart to go elsewhere. As a result, he heard a sermon on Christ's words to the disciples after the calming of the storm: "Why are you afraid, O you of little faith?"[11] He was immediately brought into a new sense of peace and assurance. The imagery of the text, as we shall see, would later echo throughout his writings.

Later that same year, he began his career as an author with the publication of a polemical work, *A Display of Arminianism*.[12] The book was dedicated to the Committee of Religion, which had begun its work as a kind of theological watchdog two years earlier. In turn, the committee appointed him the following year to serve the church at Fordham in Essex.

Now settled in pastoral ministry, Owen met and married Mary Rooke, who would bear him eleven children, only one of whom survived into adulthood. By 1646, however, his ministry at Fordham came to an end. His original appointment had been the result of the sequestration of the previous incumbent. Now the appointment of his successor reverted to the original (and non-Puritan) patron.

But John Owen had already come to public attention. He had recently been invited to preach before Parliament.[13] Now he was appointed to serve the congregation of St. Peter's, Coggeshall, also in the county of Essex.[14] This was a large

---

11. Matt. 8:26.
12. In *Works* 10:1–137.
13. On April 29, 1646. His sermon is reprinted in *Works* 8:2ff.
14. On August 18, 1646.

congregation that had recently enjoyed the distinguished ministry of Obadiah Sedgwick.[15] Here, Owen both ministered within the parish church and also gathered a fellowship along Congregationalist lines. His thinking had now developed from the more Presbyterian perspective he had earlier adopted when he had written *The Duty of Pastors and People Distinguished*[16] for his Fordham congregation.

Owen employed a wise and good principle whenever he thought through any controversial issue: he studied the strongest and best exposition of the view he opposed. In the case of church government, he had read the Congregationalist John Cotton's book *The Keyes of the Kingdom of Heaven* and found it convinced him.[17] His precise views in later life have been debated, but the indications are that he held to something like a loose form of Presbyterian-Congregationalism that both recognized that a congregation is the church in any particular place, yet, as such, wisely consults with other congregations in matters of common interest or concern.[18]

---

15. Sedgwick (1600–58) had also been a student at Queen's College, Oxford, and would later serve as a member of the Westminster Assembly.

16. In *Works* 13:3ff.

17. John Cotton, who was minister in both Boston, Lincolnshire, and later in Boston, Massachusetts, was one of the most significant and influential figures in the Puritan Brotherhood. Owen's account of his change in ecclesiology is found in *Works* 13:222–23.

18. The author of the first (anonymous) *Memoir of Owen* noted, "I heard him say, before a person of quality and others, he could readily join with Presbytery as it was exercised in Scotland." Cited in Andrew Thomson, *Life of Dr Owen*, in *Works* 1:XCVIII.

STEPPING ONTO THE NATIONAL STAGE

As events in the Civil War began to move inexorably to their climax, Owen found himself further caught up into national life. At the same time, his career began to intersect with that of Oliver Cromwell, the charismatic general who would later rule as lord protector of the Commonwealth of England, Scotland, and Ireland.

In the summer of 1648, the nearby city of Colchester[19] was under siege by General Thomas Fairfax and the Parliamentarians' New Model Army. Owen was invited to preach to the troops[20] and became a personal friend of some of the officers, including Henry Ireton, Cromwell's son-in-law.[21] Step by step, Owen was becoming a public figure.

The next year, as we have seen, he preached before Parliament the day after Charles I's execution.[22] Rather than engaging in triumphalism, Owen instead preached on the call to humility and steadfastness in the face of suffering. Three months after that momentous occasion, he was invited to preach before Parliament once again,[23] with Cromwell in the congregation.

---

19. The towns are some ten miles apart.

20. His sermons on Habakkuk 3:1–9 were later published as one under the title *Ebenezer: A Memorial of the Deliverance of Essex County, and Committee*; in *Works* 8:73.

21. Owen would later preach his funeral sermon in 1651. See *Works* 8:345–63.

22. Printed in *Works* 8:127–62. Owen has been both vilified and praised for his sermon. Perhaps the most striking feature of it is its total lack of specific reference to the events of the previous day. The sermon was, however, considered worthy to be publicly burned at Oxford on July 21, 1683, within weeks of his death.

23. This sermon, *The Shaking and Translating of Heaven and Earth*, is found in *Works* 8:244ff.

The following day, Owen visited the home of General Fairfax. While Owen waited to be seen, Cromwell and a number of his officers arrived. Recognizing Owen, Cromwell put his hand on his shoulder and said, "Sir, you are the man I must be acquainted with." Owen's (quick-thinking) response was to say, "That will be much more to my advantage than to yours!" "We shall soon see that!" Cromwell replied. He immediately invited Owen to join him in Ireland and to serve both as his chaplain and as a visitor to Trinity College, Dublin. Owen's younger brother, Philemon, already served in the army and persuaded him to accept the challenge.

Thus, Owen accompanied some twelve thousand psalm-singing soldiers in the New Model Army. Cromwell laid siege to the city of Drogheda, Ireland, which had become the focal point of resistance for Royalist opposition. When it refused to accept terms of surrender, Cromwell's army showed no quarter in taking the city. Students of history have discussed and debated both the number of civilian casualties and the ethics of Cromwell's action ever since. Owen was almost certainly not an eyewitness of the event, but his intimate knowledge of it stirred him to both high eloquence and passionate appeal when he preached before Parliament on his return:

> How is it that Jesus Christ is in Ireland only as a *lion staining all his garments with the blood of his enemies*; and none to hold him out as a *lamb sprinkled with his own blood to his friends*?

He pleaded with the members of Parliament, that

the Irish might enjoy Ireland so long as the moon endureth, so that Jesus Christ might possess the Irish. . . . I would that there were for the present one gospel preacher for every walled town in the English possession in Ireland. The land mourneth, and the people perish for want of knowledge. . . . The tears and cries of the inhabitants of Dublin after the manifestations of Christ are ever in my view.[24]

Later in 1649, Owen became an official preacher at the Palace of Whitehall,[25] and the following year he was with Cromwell again, this time on an expedition north of the border to subdue the Scots. Here Owen preached and debated repeatedly—on one occasion, according to local tradition, finding himself at least matched, if not bettered in discussion by the brilliant young theologian and minister Hugh Binning. Cromwell was sufficiently impressed to ask for his name, and discovering it was "Binning" (which may have been pronounced more like "Bunning"), he commented with a sharp pun, "He hath *bound* well, indeed" and then, putting hand to sword, added, "But *this* will *loose* all again!"[26]

---

24. *Works* 8:235–36. It seems that Owen's preaching had led to the conversion of some in Dublin.

25. The royal residence in London during the sixteenth and seventeenth centuries.

26. Hugh Binning (1627–53) was minister of Govan (now part of the city of Glasgow) and an outstandingly gifted thinker and preacher. Despite his short life, he left a remarkable collection of work, which was published posthumously.

OXFORD AND CROMWELL—AGAIN

In 1651, Owen became dean of Christ Church, Oxford, and in September the following year (contrary to Owen's personal wishes), Cromwell appointed him the university's vice-chancellor (the executive head of the university). He preached regularly in his college and also on alternate Sundays with his friend Thomas Goodwin at St. Mary's Church.[27] When not preaching at St. Mary's, he seems to have preached to familiar friends at Stadham.

It is to a sermon series from this period that we owe one of the books for which Owen is best known today, *On the Mortification of Sin*.[28] On reading this paperback-length book for the first time, most contemporary Christians are left feeling they have never read anything quite like it. That impression is deepened by the realization that Owen's profound spiritual analysis is simply the edited version of messages he had preached to a congregation composed, in large measure, of teenage students. Perhaps memories of his own earlier spiritual struggles underlined for him how important it is to go deep as early as possible. There are few things more important in the Christian life than learning to overcome sin.

---

27. Both Owen and Goodwin had been appointed heads of colleges on the same day, June 8, 1649 (Goodwin of Magdalen [pronounced "Modlin"]), and both were awarded the degree doctor of divinity in December 1653. Owen used the title *doctor* reluctantly. In 1654, he represented Oxford in Parliament (he was presumably the best-qualified person to do so) but was forced to withdraw because he was an ordained clergyman. Presumably, as a Nonconformist and an academic rather than strictly speaking a pastor, Owen was not governed by the regulation forbidding ministers from serving as members of Parliament.

28. *Works* 6:1–86.

We all have in our mind's eye a picture of a Puritan. It is often a distorted one.[29] Owen apparently did not resemble the dark misrepresentation. Indeed, the contemporary caricature of him—however overdrawn it may have been by his enemies—actually demeaned him by drawing him in bright colors. According to Anthony Wood's famous description, he

> instead of being a grave example to the University, scorned all formality, undervalued his office by going in quirpo like a young scholar, with powdered hair, snakebone bandstrings, lawn bands, a very large set of ribbons pointed at his knees, and Spanish leather boots with large lawn tops, and his hat mostly cock'd.[30]

Yet even Wood was forced to acknowledge, doubtless with a touch of cynicism:

> His personage was proper and comely and he had a very graceful behaviour in the pulpit, an eloquent elocution, a winning and insinuating deportment, and could, by the persuasion of his oratory . . . move and win the affection of his admiring auditory almost as he pleased.[31]

---

29. For a helpful corrective, see Leland Ryken, *Worldly Saints* (Grand Rapids, Mich.: Zondervan, 1986).

30. Anthony Wood, *Athenae Oxoniensis* (London, 1691), 3rd ed., ed. Philip Bliss (London, 1813–20), IV, col. 98. Cited by Thomson, *Life of Dr Owen*, in *Works* 1:XLVIII–XLIX.

31. Wood, col. 102. Cited by Toon, *God's Statesman*, p. 55.

Oxford was in a state of disarray at the end of the Civil War. Five of the colleges were deserted; some had been used largely to quarter military personnel. Owen referred to "the despised tears and sobs of our almost dying mother, the University."[32] But his administration brought fresh life into the institution, new and distinguished faculty members, and a period in which a variety of influential students would pass through its corridors of learning.[33]

His major regret from his decade in academia seems to have been that his literary output was not greater. Yet it was during this time that he published several of his most substantial works, including *The Doctrine of the Saints' Perseverance* (1654)—in essence a book review of John Goodwin's Arminian treatise *Redemption Redeemed* but one that extends to some 666 pages in the Goold edition of his *Works*. In a steady stream of literary output, there followed his defense of orthodox Christianity against Socinianism[34] in *Vindiciae*

32. William Orme, *Memoirs of the Life, Writings, and Religious Connexions of John Owen, D.D.* (London, 1810), p. 170.

33. Owen's Fifth Oration, delivered at the university convocation on October 9, 1657, is a wonderful testimony to both his Christian commitment and his administrative abilities. See *The Oxford Orations of Dr John Owen*, ed. Peter Toon (Callington, Cornwall, England: Gospel Communication, 1971), pp. 40–46. The list of students at Oxford during Owen's vice-chancellorship include John Locke, the philosopher; William Penn, founder of Pennsylvania; Christopher Wren, the great architect of the rebuilding of London; Thomas Ken, author of "The Doxology"; and many others, some of whom would lay the foundations for the Royal Society. Owen certainly held the view that Christians have a cultural mandate to explore God's creation.

34. Socinianism was a sixteenth- and seventeenth-century form of what we today would call Unitarianism, named after two of its leaders, Lelio Sozini (1525–62), who knew and corresponded with Calvin, and his nephew Fausto Sozzini (1539–1604; the nephew spelled his name with a double *z*). Socinianism developed particularly in

Evangelicae (which he dedicated to Cromwell, 1655), *Of the Mortification of Sin in Believers* (1656), *Of Communion with God the Father, Son and Holy Ghost* (1657), *Of Schism* (1657), and *Of Temptation: The Nature and Power of It* (1658). He must also have been working on his extensive Latin work *Theologoumena Pantodapa* (Theology of all kinds, 1661).

The reasons for viewing himself as a literary "underachiever" were not sloth or indifference. As he himself hinted, much of his time was taken up with affairs of state. Not only was he called on to preach before Parliament and on other civic occasions, but he also served as one of the "triers" charged with assessing fitness for gospel ministry and was frequently consulted by both politicians and pastors, and by Cromwell in particular, on matters of national and ecclesiastical importance.[35] He served in a variety of ways as a "negotiator and trouble-shooter."[36]

Poland, and its leaders expressed their beliefs in *The Racovian Catechism* (1605). An English version was produced by John Biddle and published in 1652. The catechism was burned two years later under Cromwell's administration. Owen saw Socinianism as a major enemy of the gospel and especially expounded and defended the doctrine of the priesthood of Christ against it. Cf. Sinclair B. Ferguson, introduction to *The Priesthood of Christ, Its Necessity and Nature*, by John Owen (Fearn, Ross-shire, Scotland: Christian Focus, 2010).

35. These gatherings included one convened by Cromwell himself to discuss the question of the legal residence of Jews in England. Cromwell, partly motivated by a desire for their conversion as well as their widely recognized business acumen, was in favor of allowing the Jews to remain. Owen shared Cromwell's understanding of Romans 11:25–32, although he resolutely declined to speculate on how it would take place. See *Works*, 4:440 and also 18:434 (this is volume 1 of his Hebrews commentary). Cromwell made a speech to the Council of State on December 4, 1655, on this subject that one hearer said was "the best speech he ever made." Antonia Fraser, *Cromwell, Our Chief of Men* (London: Weidenfeld and Nicolson, 1975), p. 565.

36. For a full account, see Toon, *God's Statesman*, pp. 80–102. Toon's work remains the most comprehensive modern biography.

Owen's star as vice-chancellor would, however, soon be on the wane. The Parliament that had held out so much hope to him of a nation led by genuinely Christian and Reformed leaders had, to his mind, grown spiritually tepid.

In particular, Owen was deeply troubled by and opposed to the proposals being aired in 1657 that Cromwell should become king. Cromwell was offered the throne on March 31 and wrestled with the decision for a number of weeks thereafter. In early May, he seemed to be on the verge of accepting it when his son-in-law Charles Fleetwood, Thomas Pride (who had signed the death warrant for Charles I), and others approached him personally with their objections. They called Owen into service in order to draw up a petition opposing his enthronement, and Cromwell immediately declined the throne. This marked the end of any royal aspirations Cromwell may have had. It also marked the end of Owen's ease of access to him and influence on him. More than a decade later, Owen was personally attacked by the Anglican minister George Vernon in *A Letter to a Friend concerning some of Dr Owen's Principles and Practices* (1670). Accused of promising Cromwell during his last illness that he would be raised up, Owen replied, "I saw him not in his sickness, nor in some long time before."[37] Although not involved in the installation of Cromwell as lord protector, he does seem to have had some part in Cromwell's funeral services.

---

37. *Works* 16:273–74.

Thus, Owen's leadership of the university as a whole came to an end in 1657, although he remained as dean of Christ Church until the restoration of the monarchy in 1660.

Despite his differences with the lord protector, Owen's speech on the occasion of the election of Cromwell's son, Richard, to the office of chancellor of Oxford abounds in graciousness:

> There is no need to expatiate now on his [Oliver Cromwell's] merits or to recount his benefactions when all are eager to acknowledge their debt to him for all their blessings. . . . Therefore, it is deliberately that I refrain here from giving any formal appraisal of the wisest and most gallant of all the men whom this age, rich in heroes, has produced. In whatever direction England finally moves it will go down to the ages that she had a ruler who had the glory of this island and the respect for religion close to his heart.[38]

George Vernon also accused Owen of "being the instrument in the ruining of his [Oliver Cromwell's] son" and in the failure of the Protectorate in which he followed his father. Owen was certainly close to a group of men who shared a common desire for a republic rather than a Protectorate (corporately described as "the Wallingford House Group" because of their meeting place), but he denied the charge: "with whose

---

38. Toon, ed., *The Oxford Orations of Dr John Owen*, p. 47.

[Richard Cromwell's] setting up and pulling down I had no more to do than himself."[39]

In October 1658, during his closing years at Oxford, Owen participated in a gathering of representatives of around one hundred Independent churches meeting at the Savoy Palace in London. Here, as an expression of doctrinal unity—and to a degree as a defense against the often-expressed criticism that Independency, in advocating local congregational control and rejecting church hierarchies, was a form of sectarianism that wounded the church of Christ[40]—the Independents drew up a declaration of faith with a lengthy preface probably largely written by Owen.

In great measure, the Savoy Declaration of Faith and Order adopts the text of the Westminster Confession of Faith of 1647. Its most substantial changes were in its discussion of repentance (chapter 15); the addition of an entirely new chapter 20: "Of the Gospel, and of the extent of the Grace thereof"; a rewriting of an entire section on the limits of the authority of the magistrate with respect to the church (chapter 24, section 3), and a new writing of sections 2 and 5 in the chapter on the church (chapter 26).

---

39. *Works* 16:274.

40. When a copy of the declaration was presented to Richard Cromwell on October 14, 1658, Thomas Goodwin noted in his speech, "We [desired] in the first place to clear ourselves of that scandal, which not only some persons at home, but of foreign parts, have affixed upon us, viz. that Independentism (as they call it) is the sink of all Heresies and Schisms." Quoted by A.G. Matthews in his introduction to *The Savoy Declaration of Faith and Order 1658,* ed. A.G. Matthews (London: Independent Press, 1959), p. 12.

Perhaps the most interesting change in relation to our theme is the way in which chapter 2, "Of God and of the Holy Trinity," was revised to conclude with these additional words, expressing, as we shall see, a deep Owenian conviction: "Which doctrine of the Trinity is the foundation of all our Communion with God, and comfortable Dependence upon him."[41]

THE RESTORATION AND THE EJECTION

After the execution of Charles I, Parliament abolished the monarchy and declared England to be a Commonwealth. But after Richard Cromwell failed to continue his father's success as lord protector, Parliament removed him and restored the monarchy in 1660. King Charles II, son of the king whom Parliament had executed, was crowned on April 23, 1661, at Westminster Abbey.

The Restoration ushered in difficult times for Owen and his fellow Nonconformists. A new religious settlement was now put in place and undergirded by the acts of the Clarendon Code, which placed heavy restrictions on Nonconformists:

- The Corporation Act of 1661 prohibited Nonconformists from holding civic office.
- The Act of Uniformity of 1662 excluded them from office in the church. This act led to the expulsion of some two thousand ministers from

---

41. Matthews, p. 79.

the Church of England, an event known as the Great Ejection.

- The Conventicle Act of 1662 made Nonconformist meetings illegal.
- The Five Mile Acts of 1665 prohibited Nonconformist ministers from living within five miles of any place where they had once ministered.[42]

Owen declined to conform, and thus, his service to the University of Oxford was brought to an end. He withdrew to his small estate at Stadhampton and sought to continue to minister to gathered groups of believers there and elsewhere, in contravention of the law. He did not lack opportunities to conform (he may well have been offered a bishopric) or to serve elsewhere (he was invited to follow John Cotton at the First Congregational Church of Boston, Massachusetts). He remained with others who suffered for the sake of their conviction. While not exposed to the same privations as some of his brethren, Owen and his family do seem to have moved from one house to another where they would be protected guests. For a man who had moved easily in the corridors of power, these must have been days of profound humiliation.

In 1665, England experienced the most severe outbreak of plague since the Black Death struck Europe in the fourteenth

---

42. The Clarendon Code was named after Edward Hyde, Lord Clarendon, the lord chancellor during whose administration its various laws were enacted, although he was not directly responsible for them. Cf. J.P. Kenyon, *Stuart England*, 2nd ed. (London: Penguin Books, 1985), pp. 215–16.

century. In London, about fifteen percent of the population died, including more than seven thousand in one fateful week. The plague finally ended in 1666, which was also the year of the Great Fire of London. These events were thought by many to be a divine judgment for the treatment of the Nonconformists. In any event, Owen joined many of his Puritan brethren in ministering to the needy in the city. He took this opportunity to plead for toleration in his works *Indulgence and Toleration Considered* and *A Peace Offering* (both published in 1667). He continued to work behind the scenes to secure relief for his fellow Independents. Indeed, on one occasion, he was forced to defend his actions for receiving a considerable sum of money from the Duke of York (a Roman Catholic) to alleviate the privation of suffering Dissenters. Although arrested or close to arrest on a number of occasions, he was never imprisoned.

Owen knew and greatly esteemed the suffering "Tinker-Preacher" John Bunyan, and indeed appears to have been the go-between to make arrangements for his own publisher, Nathaniel Ponder, to publish Bunyan's great work *The Pilgrim's Progress*. According to both Bunyan's and Owen's biographers, the king once asked Owen why he so appreciated an uneducated tinker like Bunyan, to which he replied, "Could I possess the tinker's abilities for preaching, please your majesty, I would gladly relinquish all my learning."[43]

---

43. Toon, *God's Statesman*, p. 162.

Faithful to the End

In 1673, the little congregation to which Owen privately ministered united with the church fellowship of which the Westminster Divine Joseph Caryl had been pastor. During this last decade of Owen's life, his time would be spent writing, preaching, and giving counsel. His first wife, Mary, died in 1675. He was married again eighteen months later, to Michel, the widow of one Thomas D'Oyley. Her companionship must have filled a great void in his life and at the same time brought much comfort in days of ongoing sickness.

Throughout these years, Owen suffered from severe asthma and gallstones, and at times was too sick to preach. He nevertheless continued to publish (almost two dozen items issued from his pen during this last decade). Even in his dying months, he was working on what by any reckoning is a classic work of theology filled with spiritual sensitivity and personal devotion, *Meditations and Discourses on the Glory of Christ*.[44]

No account of his life, however brief, would be complete without including a section of the letter he wrote to his friend Charles Fleetwood on the day before his death, and a conversation he had with a colleague on the next morning. To Fleetwood he wrote:

> I am going to Him whom my soul hath loved, or rather who hath loved me with an everlasting love;

---

44. *Works* 1:273–415.

which is the whole ground of all my consolation. The passage is very irksome and wearysome through strong pains of various sorts which are all issued in an intermitting fever. All things were provided to carry me to London today attending to the advice of my physician, but we were all disappointed by my utter disability to undertake the journey.

I am leaving the ship of the church in a storm, but whilst the great Pilot is in it the loss of a poore under-rower will be inconsiderable. Live and pray and hope and doe not despair; the promise stands invincible that he will never leave thee nor forsake thee.[45]

How fitting that in almost his last recorded words there should be a final appearance of imagery from the text that had brought him into the assurance of Christ he had now long enjoyed!

The next day, he confirmed his sense of assurance with even greater force when William Payne,[46] a minister from Saffron Waldon, visited to tell him that his *Meditations on the Glory of Christ* was at that very hour going to press. The dying Owen's response was memorable: "I am glad to hear it; but O brother Payne! The long wished for day is come at last, in which I shall see that glory in another manner than I have ever done, or was capable of doing in this world."[47]

---

45. Toon, *Correspondence*, p. 174.
46. Biographers differ on Payne's Christian name. Orme gives it as Thomas (p. 448).
47. Thomson, *Life of Dr Owen,* in *Works* 1:CIII.

By the evening of that day, August 24, 1683, St. Bartholomew's Day—twenty-one years after the ejection of two thousand ministers from the Church of England in 1662, and on the anniversary of the St. Bartholomew's Day massacre of 1572, when between five thousand and thirty thousand French Protestants were slaughtered—John Owen was with Christ. On the fourth of September, followed by a long line of stately carriages, his body was taken to Bunhill Fields, the Nonconformist burial ground then just outside the City of London. There, with the mortal remains of friends and fellow-laborers in Christ—John Bunyan, David Clarkson (once his assistant), his friend Charles Fleetwood, and many others, the dust of John Owen, pastor of Christ's flock, preacher of Christ's gospel, teacher of Christ's universal church, awaits the glory of the resurrection.

There can be no doubt, for all his massive intellect and prodigious self-discipline (how does one man write twenty-four volumes using seventeenth-century writing materials?), that the secret of Owen's life lay not in his natural gifts but in his deep devotion to God—Father, Son, and Holy Spirit. Perhaps the summary of his life that most matched his own aspirations is found in these words from a defense of Owen's character and work, *Vindication of Owen by a Friendly Scrutiny*:

His general frame was serious, cheerful, and discoursive, his expressions savouring nothing of discontent, much of heaven and love to Christ, and saints, and all men; which came from him so seriously and spontaneously, as if grace and nature were in him reconciled, and but one thing.[48]

To this day, the words of Thomas Gilbert's epitaph can be found on his gravestone:

Et, missis Caeteris, Coluit ipse, Sensitque,
Beatam quam scripsit, cum Deo Communionem
And, with a disregard for other things, he cherished
and experienced
That blessed communion with God about which he
wrote.

To the wonder of this privilege, and to Owen's unique exposition of it, we now turn.

---

48. *Vindication of Owen by a Friendly Scrutiny*, p. 38, cited by Thomson, *Life of Dr Owen*, in *Works* I:CIV–CV.

CHAPTER TWO

In the Name of the Father, Son, and Holy Spirit

[Owen's teaching on communion with the Trinity] drives one to seek the face of "God in three Persons" and to enjoy the rich fare of His "banqueting house." For those seeking assurance of their salvation it is a particularly valuable cordial.

—D. MARTYN LLOYD-JONES

Why write about communion with the Trinity? Can such a theme have any practical value for living the Christian life today?

How easily we lose sight of what is basic to the New Testament and its teaching on what it means to be a Christian. For the whole Christian life, from the outset, is lived in the light of the fact that we have been baptized "in the name of the Father and of the Son and of the Holy Spirit."[1]

---

1. Matt. 28:19.

To be a Christian is, first and foremost, to belong to the triune God and to be named for Him. This is the heart and core of the privileges of the gospel. Once we were aliens from the family of God, strangers to Christ, without desire or power to please Him. But now, through the Son whom the Father sent into the world to save us, and the Spirit who brings all the resources of Christ to us, we have come to know "the grace of the Lord Jesus Christ and the love of God [the Father] and the fellowship of the Holy Spirit."[2] To become a Christian believer is to be brought into a reality far grander than anything we could ever have imagined. It means communion with the triune God.

Yet, is it not true that, despite some signs of encouragement, many Christians rarely give much thought to the importance of God's being Trinity? Sometimes it seems that a *one-person God* is enough to satisfy us—whether that one person is Father, or Son, or Holy Spirit. Thinking of God as triune simply complicates matters. Or so it would seem, since the doctrine of the Trinity is surely (1) the most speculative and (2) the least practical of all Christian doctrines—is it not? Speculative—for how can God be three-in-one? And impractical, since it makes no real difference to day-to-day Christian living.

A Neglected Truth

Many Christians are surprised to learn the kind of company in which we find ourselves when we think in this way. For this was

---

2. 2 Cor. 13:14.

the view of the philosophers of the Enlightenment. Indeed, it is precisely the view of Immanuel Kant (1724–1804), who famously wrote: "The doctrine of the Trinity, taken literally, has *no practical relevance at all*, even if we think we understand it; and it is even more clearly irrelevant if we realize that it transcends all our concepts."[3]

A century later, Friedrich Schleiermacher (1768–1834), often called "the Father of Modern Theology," further affected the Christian church when he relegated his discussion of the Trinity to an appendix in his major work *The Christian Faith*. But what was once the position of liberal Christianity has now reappeared and has been woven into the warp and woof of evangelicalism. We live in an age that stresses practical Christian living; we have little patience for the difficult doctrine of the Trinity.

So was Kant right after all? Does the doctrine of the Trinity have "no practical relevance"?

John Owen faced similar reactions: on the one hand, attacks on the "irrational" nature of the doctrine of the Trinity, and on the other, emphasis on only one or another person (Father *or* Son *or* Holy Spirit). Yet Owen believed that rather than being speculative, the doctrine of the Trinity provided the light by which everything else became clear. Rather than being impractical, it was the most practical truth of all—for what can be more practical than knowing God in Jesus Christ and through the illuminating work of the Holy Spirit? For this

---

3. Immanuel Kant, *The Conflict of the Faculties*, trans. Mary J. Gregor (New York: Abaris Books, 1979), pp. 66–67. Italics original.

is surely the "eternal life" of which Jesus spoke: "And this is eternal life, that they know you the only true God, and Jesus Christ whom you have sent."[4]

In the light of this, it might seem puzzling that "eternal life" could be reduced to feeling peace, finding purpose, or, alas, making advance in the project of the life of the self. By contrast, Jesus Himself described it as knowing God.

This knowledge of God is our boast, Paul noted: "So that, as it is written, 'Let the one who boasts, boast in the Lord.'"[5] His words echo the great statement of Jeremiah: "Thus says the LORD: 'Let not the wise man boast in his wisdom, let not the mighty man boast in his might, let not the rich man boast in his riches, but let him who boasts boast in this, that he understands and knows me, that I am the LORD.'"[6]

Nor is this an old covenant rather than a new covenant perspective. For later, speaking again as the mouthpiece of God, Jeremiah foresees the days of the new covenant: "And no longer shall each one teach his neighbor and each his brother, saying, 'Know the LORD,' for they shall all know me. . . . For I will forgive their iniquity, and I will remember their sin no more."[7]

The forgiveness of sins we enjoy, the peace with God we receive, indeed, our justification and reconciliation are, in one sense, means to this great end—that we might know Him. This is why Paul can describe conversion in these terms: "Now

---

4. John 17:3.
5. 1 Cor. 1:31.
6. Jer. 9:23–24.
7. Jer. 31:34.

that you have come to know God."[8] This is surely why the Lord Jesus, in the darkest hours of His disciples' lives, spent time teaching them the knowledge of God, and especially the interrelationships of the Father, the Son, and the Holy Spirit, and the significance of these relationships for believers.[9]

Owen shared his Master's magnificent vision. We were made to know and love God in all His glory. To our shame, we have turned our backs on such an honor: "For although they knew God, they did not honor him as God or give thanks to him, but they became futile in their thinking, and their foolish hearts were darkened."[10]

The wonder of the gospel is that we can be restored to this high privilege as we learn what it means to "have put on the new self, which is being renewed in knowledge after the image of its creator."[11] It is not surprising, therefore, that someone as steeped in biblical thinking as John Owen would place the knowledge of God the Father, Son, and Holy Spirit at the center of his teaching.

OWEN'S ANSWERS

We would expect that John Owen would have his own answers to the two most common reasons for neglecting Trinitarian thinking and living.

---

8. Gal. 4:9.
9. See John 14–17.
10. Rom. 1:21.
11. Col. 3:10.

(1) To suggest that the Trinity is an irrational doctrine is to be guilty of making man and his reason the measure of all things. It makes the common but false philosophical assumption that God is like a man, so that whenever we speak or think about Him, we are simply attributing to Him larger versions of what is true of ourselves. But, as Karl Barth once wittily remarked, "One can *not* speak of God simply by speaking of man in a loud voice."[12]

The truth is that we are prone to looking through the wrong end of the telescope. We move from man to God. But true thinking—thinking that recognizes the real distinction between the Creator and the creature, between the Infinite and the finite—must always begin with God. It is not so much that we describe God in *anthropomorphic* terms; it is that He has created us in a *theomorphic* way. We are the miniatures. In us—created, finite people—are embedded microcosmic reflections of realities that are true of God Himself in a macrocosmic, uncreated, infinite way.

Owen grasped this, and says (in an admittedly intellectually challenging statement): "In one essence there can be but one person, may be true where the substance is finite and limited, but hath no place in that which is infinite."[13]

From a creaturely perspective, therefore, God's Trinitarian being is therefore not to be thought of as *irrational*, but as

---

12. Karl Barth, *The Word of God and the Word of Man*, trans. D. Horton (New York: Harper and Row, 1957), p. 196.

13. John Owen, *On Communion with God the Father, Son, and Holy Ghost, each person distinctly, in love, grace, and consolation; or, The Saints' Fellowship with the Father, Son, and Holy Ghost Unfolded*, in *Works* 2:388.

suprarational. What is beyond human reason is not necessarily contradictory to true and ultimate reason. The finite mind cannot comprehend Infinite Mind. While we can *apprehend* God's Godness, it is clear that we cannot fully *comprehend* it. To think otherwise would be to fall under Martin Luther's criticism of the prominent humanist Desiderius Erasmus (1466–1536): "Your thoughts of God are too human."[14]

There are places in our quest for understanding where we reach the limits of the human mind. The finite does not have the capacity fully to grasp and understand the infinite. But it is how we respond just at this point that is significant. Do we say with Nietzsche, "But to reveal my entire heart to you, my friends, *if* there were gods, how could I stand not to be a god! *Therefore*, there are no gods."[15] Or do we bow down, "lost in wonder, love, and praise,"[16] because we recognize we have come to the horizon of human understanding and can only gaze in awe at the God who is so infinitely great and glorious—and who loves and cares for us? Therein lies the difference between the approach of alienation and the approach of faith.

(2) But Owen is concerned to take us beyond intellectual controversy. For far from seeing the Trinity as an impractical

---

14. Martin Luther, *On the Bondage of the Will*, in *Luther and Erasmus*, eds. E. Gordon Rupp and Philip S. Watson (Philadelphia: Westminster Press, 1969), p. 125.

15. Friedrich Nietzsche, *Thus Spake Zarathustra*, eds. Adrian Del Caro and Robert Pippin, Cambridge Texts in the History of Philosophy (Cambridge, England: Cambridge University Press, 2006), p. 65. Italics original.

16. From the hymn "Love Divine, All Loves Excelling" by Charles Wesley (1707–88).

and abstract doctrine, it is for him—by necessity—the most practical of all doctrines, simply because knowing God *is* eternal life.

But before we begin to explore its implications in detail, we must look at how Owen understands the Bible's teachings on the Trinity.

ON THE TRINITY

Owen stands unashamedly on the shoulders of multitudes of Christians before him. He sees that the biblical teaching is in fact very straightforward: God is one.[17] Yet the Father, the Son, and the Holy Spirit are each seen as divine. Not only is the Father Himself God, but the New Testament applies to Jesus quotations from the Old Testament that in their original context clearly refer to the Divine Being.[18] In addition, divine and personal attributes and actions are attributed to the Holy Spirit.

This is why Christians are baptized into the *one* name that has the threefold pronunciation "Father, Son, and Holy Spirit."[19] Here Owen has a new twist on an observation made by the early church father Athanasius to the effect that if the Son and the Spirit are not divine, then we are inexplicably baptized in the name of one God and two creatures. Owen notes, "If those into whose name we are baptized be not one in nature,

17. Deut. 6:4; Isa. 44:6, 8.
18. See *Works* 2:323–26 for what Owen calls "some" of these passages.
19. Matt. 28:18–20.

we are by our baptism engaged into the service and worship of more gods than one."[20]

But how is this a *practical* doctrine? For Owen, this is like asking how marriage is a practical arrangement. The presence and character of our marriage partner changes absolutely everything!

He develops two aspects of Trinitarian theology first expounded by the church fathers. The first is the doctrine of the works of the Trinity (*opera Trinitatis*). The second is the doctrine of the appropriations of the persons of the Trinity (*appropriationes personae*).

These expressions may sound obscure and complex. But they are actually very beautiful doctrines, and they open up for us in a wonderful way what it means to know God and help us to enjoy fellowship with Him.

Opera Trinitatis ad extra sunt indivisa

This grand-sounding sentence is translatable with little or no knowledge of Latin: the external works of the Trinity are indivisible. This is another way of saying that when God acts, He always acts as God the Trinity. The fathers of the church had a corresponding statement with respect to God's inner being as Trinity,[21] implying that communications of love between any of the divine persons always engage all three persons. Paul's statement that "the Spirit searches everything, even the

---

20. *Works* 2:405.
21. *Opera Trinitatis ad intra sunt indivisa.*

depths of God"[22] implies as much. It means that when Jesus spoke about the Father's love for the Son and the Son's love for the Father, He did not exclude the Spirit from the mutual embrace. Indeed, Augustine had taught that in some sense the Spirit *is* the bond of that embrace.

In all God's actions and expressions of love and purpose toward the cosmos, and especially toward men and women made in His image, each person of the Trinity is engaged. This is especially clear in His epoch-making actions of creation and incarnation.

The Father is the Creator, and yet He makes all things through His Son, the Word, without whom "was not any thing made that was made."[23] But already in Genesis 1:2, we read of the Spirit of God hovering over the waters as the divine executive who superintended the original formless, empty, dark creation in order to bring forth both form and fullness in the light of God.

Later, the Father sent His Son. The Son willingly came to take our flesh and bear our sins. He was conceived in the womb of the Virgin Mary. Likewise, in the resurrection, the Father raised the Son. The Son stepped forth from the tomb, but He did so in the power of the Spirit. He was "declared to be the Son of God in power according to the Spirit of holiness by his resurrection from the dead."[24] Like others before him,[25] Owen

---

22. 1 Cor. 2:10.
23. John 1:3.
24. Rom. 1:4.
25. Calvin cites the same words from Gregory's *On Holy Baptism*, Oration 40.41, in *Institutes* 1.13.17.

was impressed by the beautiful statement of Gregory of Nazianzus: "I cannot think about the One without being instantly surrounded by the splendour of the Three, nor can I discern the Three without being immediately drawn back to the One."[26]

These three, Owen says, "thus *know* each other, *love* each other, *delight* in each other."[27] It is not surprising then that Augustine wrote: "In no other subject is error more dangerous, or inquiry more laborious, or the discovery of truth more profitable."[28] There is mystery here, but it is the mystery of infinite glory and leads to humble adoration and devotion.

But there is a further aspect to the classical doctrine of the Trinity that Owen calls into service. It is this second dimension that he develops in unusual if not unique detail, in such a way as to lead us into a deeper appreciation of what it means to know God. This is the doctrine of *appropriations*.

Appropriationes Personae

If the doctrine of the *opera Trinitatis* underscores the *unity* of the Trinity, the doctrine of the *appropriations* underscores the diversity of role and functions among Father, Son, and

---

26. Owen cites Gregory's words in *Works* 2:10, n. 1, alongside the words of Tertullian in his treatise *Against Praxeas* to the effect that the Father is one and the Son is one not by division but distinction. Praxeas was an early heretic who adopted the modalistic monarchian view that the Father, the Son, and the Holy Spirit were simply "modes" or appearances of the One. Tertullian famously noted that "Praxeas at Rome managed two pieces of the Devil's business: he drove out prophecy and introduced heresy; he put to flight the Paraclete and crucified the Father"; *Against Praxeas*, ch. 1.

27. *Works* 2:406.

28. Augustine, *On the Trinity* 1.3.

Holy Spirit. The doctrine means that each person expresses His specific personhood both internally (in relation to the other persons) and externally (in relation to the cosmos and especially mankind).

There is a deep relationship between the dispositions and actions of each person of the Trinity and the nature of the Christian's knowledge of and fellowship with that person. Our experience of the Father, the Son, and the Holy Spirit is shaped by the specific role that each plays in relationship to our lives and especially to our salvation.

This simple—but stretching to the mind and affections—truth can be simply illustrated by the confusion of speech we sometimes hear when listening to someone else pray. Either by accident, thoughtlessness, or sometimes ignorance, a person will address God as "Our Father" in prayer and thank Him for all He has done. But then, perhaps losing the thread of what he is praying, he then thanks the Father for, among other things, "dying on the cross for us." Unwittingly, he has become guilty of a well-known heresy with a sophisticated Latinate title, "patripassianism."[29]

The Father did not suffer and die for us on the cross. It was His Son, Jesus Christ, who did that. While it is certainly appropriate (and more than appropriate) to praise the Father for *sending* His Son to die for us, a moment's reflection will confirm that the Father Himself did not die.

---

29. The heresy associated with Praxeas in which the One (and therefore the Father) suffered on the cross.

Before we move on, it is worth pausing to reflect on some of the practical implications of what has just been said. For if neither the Father nor the Spirit died for us on the cross, that means it is only the Son we praise for making such a sacrifice. We have unique reasons for thanking Him (in distinction from the Father and the Spirit), which means there is a unique element to our fellowship or communion with Him. Yet, at the same time, this also suggests that there are also unique elements in our communion with the Father ("Father, thank you for *sending* your own Son for me") and with the Holy Spirit ("Holy Spirit, thank you for being with and sustaining the Lord Jesus when He died for me on the cross"[30]).

This is an ever-expanding insight. The more we reflect on the way Scripture details the activities of the Father, the Son, and the Spirit, the correspondingly fuller and richer our communion with God will become. It will no longer be communion with an undifferentiated being, but fellowship with a deeply personal, indeed three-personal, Being in all that He is in His three persons, each one in the undivided Three making Himself known to us in special and distinct ways.

THE LIVING GOD

This, for John Owen, lay at the heart of what it means to know God and to enjoy communion with Him.[31] Just as it is

---

30. See Hebrews 9:14 for this.
31. Thomas Goodwin—Owen's friend, fellow Independent, and preaching colleague at St. Mary's, Oxford—shared the same perspective: "Sometimes a man's

inconceivable that a unitarian God could enjoy personal communion within His own being, so it is inconceivable that a Christian can enjoy communion with a God who has all kinds of attributes but can never express them within His own being. Such a god is not a living god at all, but is impersonal and static.

By contrast, the God of the Bible is the living God—living in Himself, loving within His three persons, expressing all His attributes in the dynamic interplay of Father with Son, Son with Spirit, Spirit with Father, Father and Son with Spirit, Spirit and Son with Father, Father and Spirit with Son. This is what the Greek fathers of the church called *perichōrēsis* —the moving in and out (as in a choreographed dance) of the Father, the Son, and the Holy Spirit in an eternal, self–sufficient inner cosmos of love and holy devotion, and in an endless mutual knowledge.

Perhaps the nearest we get to experiencing this is in the

---

communion and converse is with the one, sometimes with the other; sometimes with the Father, then with the Son, and then with the Holy Ghost; sometimes his heart is drawn out to consider the Father's love in choosing, and then the love of Christ in redeeming, and so the love of the Holy Ghost, that searcheth the deep things of God, and revealeth them to us, and taketh all the pains with us; and so a man goes from one witness to another distinctly, which, I say, is the communion that John would have us to have." *Of the Object and Acts of Justifying Faith*, 2.2.6, in *The Works of Thomas Goodwin*, ed. Thomas Smith (Edinburgh, Scotland: James Nichol, 1864), 8:378–79. Goodwin notes this in the broader context of a discussion of the assurance of salvation. It would be interesting to speculate on what conversations passed between these two outstanding figures during their time together in Oxford as academic leaders and fellow preachers. Unfortunately, neither one left any record of their relationship. While they clearly share a common perspective here, as in other matters (they were both Congregationalists), only Owen devoted extensive exposition to the nature of this Trinitarian communion.

discovery of a friendship or love in which we seem both to lose and find ourselves in the apparently unending fascination and satisfaction of knowing and being known, loving and being loved, by another person. Time itself seems either to stand still or to become like an unending stream; being seems far more significant than doing; being *together* becomes an all-absorbing, all-consuming, all-demanding delight.

John Owen had begun to learn from the Apostles that deep down at the foundation of knowing God, and living and enjoying the Christian life, lay the experience of these basic truths:

> But when the fullness of time had come, God sent forth his Son, born of woman, born under the law, to redeem those who were under the law, so that we might receive adoption as sons. And because you are sons, God has sent the Spirit of his Son into our hearts, crying, "Abba! Father!"[32]

> Go therefore and make disciples of all nations, baptizing them in the name of the Father and of the Son and of the Holy Spirit.[33]

> Indeed, our fellowship is with the Father and with His Son, Jesus Christ.[34]

---

32. Gal. 4:4–6.
33. Matt. 28:19.
34. 1 John 1:3.

The grace of the Lord Jesus Christ and the love of God and the fellowship of the Holy Spirit be with you all.[35]

This, then, says Owen,

farther drives on the truth that lies under demonstration; there being such a distinct communication of grace from the several persons of the Deity, *the saints must needs have distinct communion with them.*[36]

To the rich wonder of this communion with each person of the Trinity we must now turn.

CHAPTER THREE

Communion with the Father

I am quite aware that Owen's writings are not fashionable in the present day. . . . Yet the great divine . . . [has] more learning and sound knowledge of Scripture in his little finger than many who depreciate him have in their whole bodies. I assert unhesitatingly that the man who wants to study experimental theology will find no books equal to those of Owen.[1]

—J.C. RYLE

Communion with God is always the enjoyment of the whole Godhead. Yet, as we have seen, it is also the enjoyment of each person. There is a distinct "flavor" about our fellowship with the Father, with the Son, and with the Holy Spirit.

---

1. J.C. Ryle, *Holiness: Its Nature, Hindrances, Difficulties, and Roots* (Cambridge, England: James Clarke, 1952), p. 33.

THE CENTRALITY OF LOVE

Christians enjoy fellowship with the Father *in love*. Yes, Scripture speaks of the love of Jesus, the Son, and also of the Holy Spirit as the One who pours the love of God into our hearts. But it places special emphasis on the love of the Father that flows to us through the Son and the Spirit. Thus, when John writes "God is love,"[2] it is the love of God the Father that he particularly has in view, since he goes on to explain how this love has been made known to us in the way "God [i.e. the Father] sent his only Son into the world."[3]

God the Father is characterized by His infinitely gracious, tender, compassionate, and loving nature. This, Owen says, "is the great *discovery* of the gospel."[4] Outside of Christ, we know God only as full of wrath; we cannot think of Him in any other way. Of course, people will say that they "believe in a God of love." But apart from Christ, this is either self-deceit or borrowed capital from the gospel. For apart from Christ, we can have no sure confidence of God's love. Providence is too mixed with tragedy, and history is too marred by evil for us to be able to read off its pages "God is love." If we believe that He is love on the grounds that things are going well for us, our confidence will dissolve the moment life turns sour. No; outside of Christ, the conviction that God is love is a figment

---

2. 1 John 4:8.
3. 1 John 4:9.
4. *Works* 2:19.

44

of our imagination. The truth is that, outside of Christ, there lies only judgment and wrath.

But the gospel gloriously affirms the love the Father has for lost sinners.[5] He is the One who sent His Son so that we should not perish but have everlasting life[6]; He is the One in whom we find the benediction of His love.[7] This was the message that the Savior emphasized to His disciples before His passion and death: "The Father himself loves you."[8]

Clearly, this love neither exists nor is manifested apart from the Son: "God shows his love for us in that while we were still sinners, Christ died for us."[9] Nor do we experience it apart from the Holy Spirit. For "God's love [i.e. the Father's love] has been poured into our hearts through the Holy Spirit who has been given to us."[10] Nevertheless, these streams of love flow to us from a fountain in God the Father.

"All you need is love." That is true, in one sense. But *love* is a multifaceted term, a comprehensive description used in Scripture for a multidimensional reality. I love theology, I love my wife, I love my family, I love golf, and I love God. Not only is that listing not in order of priority, but my "love" in each instance has a distinct flavor, a different nuance ranging from "enjoy" to "adore." So what do we mean when we speak

---

5. Owen provides a beautiful exposition of this theme in *Works* 2:19–22.

6. See John 3:16.

7. See 2 Corinthians 13:14.

8. John 16:27.

9. Rom. 5:8.

10. Rom. 5:5.

about the love of God? We need to use a variety of categories if we are going to describe how God loves.

MAKING DISTINCTIONS

In common with other theologians who tried to think through such issues, and to make careful analytical distinctions, Owen employed a series of categories to distinguish the ways we love, and especially the ways in which God loves: the love of benevolence, the love of beneficence, and the love of complacence.

These categories were well summarized and described by Owen's younger contemporary the Genevan theologian Francis Turretin (1623–87):

A threefold love of God is commonly held; or rather there are three degrees of one and the same love. First, there is the love of benevolence by which God willed good to the creature from eternity; second, the love of beneficence by which he does good to the creature in time according to his good will; third, the love of complacency by which he delights himself in the creature on account of the rays of his image seen in them. . . . By the first, he elects us; by the second, he redeems and sanctifies us; but by the third he gratuitously rewards us as holy and just. Jn. 3.13 refers to the first; Eph. 5.25 and Rev. 1.5 to the second; Is. 62.3 and Heb. 11.6 to the third.[11]

11. Francis Turretin, *Institutes of Elenctic Theology*, trans. George M. Giger, ed. James T.

Owen uses this kind of categorization in expressions such as the love of good pleasure, the love of rest and complacency, the love of friendship, the love of assimilation, the love of approbation, and so on.

Such "divisions" seem both frustrating and needlessly scholastic to many Christians. *Scholastic* is often used as a theological slur intended to introduce a bad odor. Yet the people who use it thus are sometimes the very people who become hot under the collar if strangers refer to a fastball as a "slider" (in baseball) or confuse an eagle with a double bogey (in golf) or, for that matter, describe someone living in the Carolinas as a "Yankee" or a Scot as "English"! Aren't these merely "scholastic" distinctions? To ask the question is to answer it. Right understanding always involves making careful distinctions.

Of course, we must never substitute distinctions for the thing itself; we must always recognize that distinctions are simply useful ways of helping us grasp and understand the whole. This is true with the love of the Father. It is not an amorphous concept: "God loves you." Owen teaches us to linger over His love, to meditate on its multifaceted nature in order to appreciate its wonder.

Thus, according to Owen, we must reflect on the love He had for us before we were born, and the purposes He then planned for our lives (the love of benevolence). This divine love stretches back into eternity and downwards into time.

Dennison Jr. (Phillipsburg, N.J.: Presbyterian and Reformed, 1992), vol. 1, p. 242, Q. 20.V.

Then there is the love that He has displayed in history in doing good to all people (the love of beneficence). And then there is the love, planned in eternity and expressed in Christ, that we have now come to experience (the love of complacency). It cost Him dearly to love us as sinners, for it required His willingness to send His Son and give Him up to the death of the cross in order to fulfill His purposes of love for us. We know that He loved us, but more than that, we now experience the love with which He loved us. He loves us with it still. Indeed, the Father Himself loves us![12] What knowledge could be more wonderful than this? The Father comes to make His home with us.[13]

Soul Sickness and Gospel Medicine

John Owen was a great multilingual and multidisciplinary scholar. But during much of his life, he served either as a pastor of local congregations or in pastoral relationships with others. In addition, his spiritual pilgrimage had been by no means straightforward. His experience and his calling combined to make him deeply sensitive to a spiritual condition he observed as troubling many Christians. The observations of pastors before and since simply confirm Owen's judgment that there is a spiritual sickness that often spoils our enjoyment of fellowship with God.

---

12. See John 16:27.
13. See John 14:23.

In his early years, Owen appears to have been troubled about his relationship to God. There is some evidence that he went through more than one period of spiritual discouragement and even depression. His first deliverance from this came, as we have seen, when a stranger substituted for Edmund Calamy and preached on Jesus' words to His disciples: "Why are you afraid, O you of little faith?"[14] The sermon was the means of "leading him forth into the sunshine of a settled peace."[15] But it was also probably the reason why Owen developed a lifelong concern for others who had little or no sense of peace with God.

Owen refers to this problem several times in the context of his exposition of communion with the Father *in love*. The problem as he sees it—surely rightly—is that many Christians, in their heart of hearts, are not deeply convinced that the Father indeed loves them. An extended quotation from Owen will make his point clear:

There is a twofold divine love, *beneplacti* and *amicitiae*, a love of good pleasure and destination, and a love of friendship and approbation, they are both peculiarly assigned to the Father in an eminent manner:—

John iii.16, "God so loved the world that he gave," etc.; that is with the love of his purpose and good pleasure, his determinate will of doing good. This

---

14. Matt. 8:26.
15. Thomson, *Life of Dr Owen*, in *Works* 1:XXXI.

is distinctly ascribed to him, being laid down as the cause of sending his Son. . . .

John xiv.23, there is mention of that other kind of love whereof we speak. "If a man love me," saith Christ, "he will keep my words: and my Father will love him, and we will come unto him, and make our abode with him." The love of friendship and approbation is here eminently ascribed to him. Says Christ, "We will come," even Father and Son, "to such a one and dwell with him;" that is, by the Spirit: but yet he (Jesus) would have us take notice, that, in point of love, the Father hath a peculiar prerogative: "My Father will love him."

6. Yea, and as this love is peculiarly to be eyed in him, so it is to be looked on as the *fountain* of all following gracious dispositions. *Christians walk oftentimes with exceedingly troubled hearts, concerning the thoughts of the Father towards them. They are well persuaded of the Lord Christ and his good-will; the difficulty lies in what is their acceptance with the Father.*[16]

From time to time in the enormous mass of Owen's writings, one catches a sense of passionate relentlessness. He will not let go of a theme until he has exhausted it. This is one of those places. Owen is like a physician facing an almost

16. *Works* 2:21–22. Italics mine.

intractable disease who is determined to find a diagnosis and then prescribe a cure.

What, exactly, is the problem here? There are Christians who are not deeply convinced of the love that their heavenly Father has for them. They may grasp the love of Christ, but there seems to be a cognitive gap or a dissonance between their trust in Him and their trust in the Father. It is almost as though they fear that behind Christ, the Father is actually distant and dark, even sinister:

> Many dark and disturbing thoughts are apt to arise in this thing. *Few can carry up their hearts and minds to this height by faith, as to rest their souls in the love of the Father; they live below it in the troublesome region of hopes and fears, storms and clouds.* All here is serene and quiet. But how to attain to this pitch they know not.[17]

Again, later on, Owen circles the wagons one more time:

> How few of the saints are experimentally acquainted with this privilege of holding immediate communion with the Father in love. With what anxious, doubtful thoughts do they look upon him! What fears, what questionings are there, of his good-will and kindness. *At the best, many think there is no sweetness at all in him towards us, but what is purchased at the high price*

---

17. *Works* 2:23. Italics mine.

of the blood of Jesus. It is true, that alone is the way of communication; but the free fountain and spring of all is in the bosom of the Father. [18]

What is the problem Owen detects? We might call it "serpent theology," for the record of the first attack on the relationship between God and His image-bearing son and daughter has this in view.

What is the nature of the attack? In formal terms, the serpent's words cast doubt on the content, truthfulness, and reliability of God's word: "Did God actually say . . . ?" And when Eve responds that God had said they would die if they ate of the fruit of the Tree of Knowledge of Good and Evil: "The serpent said to the woman, 'You will not surely die.'"

But woven into the serpent's approach is a more subtle activity rooted in a more sinister motive. His *twisting of the word of God* is designed to *distort the character of God* in Eve's eyes. God had given them the fruit of all the trees in the garden to enjoy. [19] Only one tree in the entire orchard was forbidden. This was overwhelmingly generous, and a simple, easily managed negative command. Clearly, the heavenly Father wanted His children to show their love, trust, and obedience to Him by simply doing what He told them. In this way, they would grow strong in faith as they gave glory to God. [20] Obedience to His command could only strengthen their trust and love.

---

18. *Works* 2:31–32. Italics mine.
19. Explicitly and specifically stated in Genesis 2:16.
20. See Romans 4:20.

But the serpent adeptly twisted the command: "He said to the woman, 'Did God actually say, "You shall not eat of any tree in the garden"?'"[21] How mean and despicable if He had issued such a command! But the serpent's question was, of course, a subtle but hate-motivated innuendo intended to distort the character and motives of the great, gracious, kind, generous Creator. "He doesn't really love you" was the implication. He was encouraging them to complain to God, "You never give us anything to enjoy!" Alas, despite Eve's initial rejoinder, the serpent succeeded.

The upshot was this: "They exchanged the truth about God for a lie."[22] The lie was this: "The Father doesn't really love you. In fact, He is malevolent toward you; He begrudges you any enjoyment, restricts your life, and, in a word, is a hard taskmaster." The consequence of Eve's dismal failure was the entry into the human psyche, now distorted by sin and the fall, of a twisted and perverse view of the character of God. Now He has become policeman, spoiler, divine Scrooge.[23] His honor and glory are now seen, by definition, as the enemy of our freedom and joy.

Yes, people will tell us they believe in a "God of love." But they are self-deceived, and their lives reveal it. They neither love Him with heart, soul, mind, and strength in return, nor do they worship Him with zeal and energy. The truth is that

21. Gen. 3:1.
22. Rom. 1:25.
23. See *Works* 2:35.

53

their mantra "My God is a God of love" is a smokescreen, a phantasm of their imagination. Underneath it all is a deep mistrust of God—otherwise, why not yield the whole of life in joyful abandon to whatever He says or asks?

Christ gives us hints of how well He Himself understood this. The returning prodigal in the parable[24] spends the journey home rehearsing his speech: "Treat me as one of your hired servants." He does not expect to see his aged father gathering up his robes and breaching social etiquette by running down the hill, embracing and kissing him, and then celebrating his return. No; righteous Jewish etiquette required a shaming ceremony, not a homecoming party. The stay-at-home, never-do-anything-wrong older son shares the same spirit: "Look, these many years I have served you . . . yet you never gave me a young goat, that I might celebrate with my friends," he complains. He sees himself as a slave, not as a son. He has no sense of the father's love.

Strikingly, Jesus paints a picture of the same spirit in His parable of the minas, in which the servant, rather than using his master's wealth productively, returns it still in the handkerchief in which he had hidden it. Why? "I was afraid of you, because you are a severe man. You take what you did not deposit, and reap what you did not sow."[25] He says this to the master who has just told the servant who turned his mina into five minas that he will become mayor of five cities. The only relationship

24. Luke 15:11–32.
25. Luke 19:21.

between five minas and five cities is the number five. This is reward out of all proportion to accomplishment. He is hardly a severe man; indeed, he is the most generous of masters!

Yet, this is our natural condition. This is how we think of the Father. Our hearts are closed to Him because we think His heart is closed to us. Owen sees this with great clarity. Moreover, he knows that this mistrust may not be entirely dissolved by regeneration. It lingers on and plagues many Christians still. It has been a lifelong addiction; it may remain an ongoing tendency. The seed of this disease of the soul is already in us and may flare up again and again.

But there is more, and Owen has hinted at it in words already quoted: "What fears, what questionings are there, of his good-will and kindness. *At the best, many think there is no sweetness at all in him towards us, but what is purchased at the high price of the blood of Jesus.*"[26]

It is true that the blood of Jesus alone is the means of communication; but the free fountain and spring of love is in the bosom of the Father. But why is it, then, that people think less of the Father's love? It is in part because sometimes this is how the gospel is preached: "God loves you, because His Son, Jesus, died for you. So trust Him as your Savior."

But, in fact, this is not how the New Testament presents the gospel. This popular presentation misrepresents the gospel; it turns it on its head, and feeds mistrust of the Father. It implies the very thing Owen believed to be so damaging to

---

26. *Works* 2.32. Italics mine.

the soul's relationship to God, namely, the belief that "there is no sweetness at all in him [the Father] towards us, but what is purchased at the high price of the blood of Jesus." Here, a loving Savior is seen to persuade a reluctant, even bitter, Father to be gracious. Jesus buys His Father's love at infinite cost.

But contrast this with the gospel teaching:

> God so loved the world, that he gave his only Son [therefore, by definition "God" here means "the Father"], that whoever believes in him should not perish but have eternal life.[27]
>
> God shows his love for us in that while we were still sinners, Christ died for us.[28]

There is no gap between the love of the Father and that of the Son. Christ died for us *because* the Father loves us, not in order to induce or persuade a reluctant Father to love us. All the love for us that we see in Jesus is the Father's love too. Yes, it is *expressed by* and *revealed in* the death of Christ, but it is not *purchased by* it. Indeed, the Father's love is antecedent to the work of Christ. The Father's love is the *sine qua non* of the work of Christ for us. For "the Father himself loves you."[29]

It is not surprising that when this malaise remains in the soul, the joy, peace, energy, worship, and witness of the

---

27. John 3:16.
28. Rom. 5:8. Verse 10 makes clear that here "God" is a reference to God the Father.
29. John 16:27.

Christian are all adversely affected. Spiritual anemia is the result. Owen, therefore, wants to prescribe medicine for sick Christian hearts—a gospel tonic that will put us on our feet and fill us with joy and assurance.

What do we need? We need to take daily doses of the Father's love and reflect on the high privilege of being His adopted children. Jesus is the beam, but the Father Himself is the sun of eternal love. Christ is the stream, but through Him we are led to the Father, who is the fountain of all grace and kindness. "He is as a father, a mother, a shepherd, a hen over chickens, and the like."[30]

How is the remedy to be taken? And how will it restore us to the wonder of communion with God the Father? Owen's prescription is that we must first receive, and then return, the Father's love.

THE RECEPTION AND RETURN OF LOVE

We receive the Father's love by faith. He has demonstrated His love in Christ. In love, He sent His Son for us. By Christ's death, all cause for the Father's wrath against us is removed. If the Father did not spare His Son, but gave Him up to the cross for us, we can reach only one conclusion: the Father will graciously supply all of our needs. We have every reason to trust Him. Not only so, but God's love for us is not limited to *benefaction*, the plan of salvation designed to do us good. It is

---

30. *Works* 2:22.

also a love of *complacency* (in the word's original sense of "satisfaction"). This is implied in the apparent mixing of metaphors in the words of Zephaniah 3:17:

> The LORD your God is in your midst,
> a mighty one who will save;
> he will rejoice over you with gladness;
> he will quiet you by his love;
> he will exult over you with loud singing.

Thus, our task is to "eye" the Father's love.

Our problem has been that our gaze has been fixed either on our own sin (we are unlovely and unlovable), or like a person with a squint, we have looked past, rather than at, the love of our Father.[31] Instead, we are meant to fix our eyes on Christ, so that they may be raised through Him to the Father's love that is demonstrated in Him. To change the metaphor, we are to drink so deeply of God's love in Christ that we reach the head of the waters found in the heart of the Father. When the eye of faith sees the Father's love, the mouth of faith will drink deeply of the streams of grace. As we do so, we not only receive His love, but we also find ourselves inevitably, irresistibly, returning His love. And, wonderfully, just as Christ is the One through whom the Father's love comes to us, so in Christ our love is returned to the Father.

---

31. Cf. the words of John Cotton in his commentary on 1 John 2:1. John Cotton, *A Commentary Upon the First Epistle General of John* (London: Thomas Parkhurst, 1658).

It should not escape our notice that this, in turn, takes place through the ministry of the Holy Spirit. Here, the choreography of the Trinity brings love down from heaven to earth, and then, as though the music accompanying the dance of grace now indicates that the direction of the dance is reversed, our love is returned to the Father through the Son by the inner ministry of the Spirit.

Yes, the Father's love for us, and ours for Him, differ. His is a love of bounty; ours is a love of duty (albeit love, not duty, is its motive). His love is antecedent to ours; our love is consequent to His. Our love goes to Him although we were once haters of God; His has come to us because He is a lover of man. We love the Lord *because* He has first loved us. His love is, like Him, unchanging and unchangeable; ours is mutable. He may not always smile out His love to us, but He never ceases actually to love us.[32]

If only we contemplated ("eyed") this love clearly, Owen comments, our souls "could not bear an hour's absence from him."[33] For this is the love of

the all sufficient, infinitely satiated [satisfied] with himself and his own glorious excellencies and perfections; who hath no need to go forth with his love unto others, nor to seek an object of it without [outside] himself. . . . He is sufficient unto his own love. He

32. *Works* 2:28–30.
33. *Works* 2:32.

59

had his Son also, his eternal Wisdom, to rejoice and delight himself in from all eternity. This might take up and satiate the whole delight of the Father.[34]

But, Owen adds: "he will love his saints also." This is, indeed, free love. There is nothing in us that causes it. It is from Him alone.

Thus, delivered from the deceit of Satan, we grow in communion with our heavenly Father, and discover with David: "So I have looked upon you in the sanctuary. . . . Because your steadfast love is better than life, my lips will praise you. So I will bless you as long as I live; in your name I will lift up my hands."[35] Thus, "When the soul sees God, in his dispensation of love, to be infinitely lovely and loving, rests upon him and delights in him as such—then hath it communion with him in love."[36]

Now that he has taught us thus to delight in our Father's love, Owen wants to lead us on further. For in Jesus Christ, there is "grace upon grace."

---

34. *Works* 2:32.
35. Ps. 63:2–4.
36. *Works* 2:24.

CHAPTER FOUR

Communion with the Son

> *Dr. Owen's is indeed a venerated name, which stands in
> the first rank of those noble worthies who adorned a former
> period of our country and of our church. He was a star of
> the first magnitude in that bright constellation of lumi-
> naries, who shed a light and a glory on the age in which
> they lived; and whose genius, and whose writings, con-
> tinue to shed their radiance over succeeding generations.*[1]
>
> —THOMAS CHALMERS

G od the Father calls us "into the fellowship of his Son,
 Jesus Christ our Lord."[2] Paul's words of thanksgiving
for God's work among the Corinthians seem so simple, so
commonplace, that it would be easy for us to take them for
granted and gloss over them. But for John Owen, the Apostle's

---

1. *Select Works of Thomas Chalmers*, vol. 1 (Minneapolis: Robert Carter, 1848), p. 262.
2. 1 Cor. 1:9.

statement serves as the open door into all the treasures of grace and blessing that are ours through faith. All that God has for us in His Son Jesus is condensed in this apparently simple statement. For to become a Christian means to have fellowship with Christ in all that He has accomplished for us. Indeed, Christ Himself invites us to "sit with him and sup with him."[3] This is what Paul prays will be ours in his Trinitarian benediction: "the grace of the Lord Jesus Christ."[4]

GRACE AND JUSTIFICATION

But what *is* this grace? From one perspective, it is the fulfillment of everything to which the Old Testament pointed in its patterns, promises, types, and history. "The law was given through Moses," John explained, but "grace and truth came through Jesus Christ."[5] It is not that the old covenant was devoid of grace. But true, real, full, embodied grace came only in the One whom the old covenant anticipated.

Owen, however, presents us with a vital additional emphasis. It ranks among one of the most important insights in all of his theology. Grace is, ultimately, personal. Grace is Jesus Christ; Jesus Christ is God's grace. For *grace* is not substantial in the sense of being a quality or entity that can be abstracted from the person of the Savior. Indeed, Owen says:

---

3. The allusion is to Revelation 3:10.

4. 2 Cor. 13:14.

5. John 1:17.

Paul is so delighted with this [the grace of Christ] that he makes it his motto, and the token whereby he would have his epistles known, 2 Thess. iii.17, 18, "The salutation of Paul with mine own hand, which is the token in every epistle; so I write. The *grace* of our Lord Jesus Christ be with you all." Yea, he makes these two, "*Grace be with you*," and, "The *Lord Jesus be with you*" to be equivalent expressions.[6]

It would be hard to overestimate the importance of these words. Owen was writing against the background of the theological categories employed in medieval theology (many of which he inherited). The medieval understanding of salvation was dominated by sacramental grace, from its first "infusion" at baptism until its hoped-for conclusion in a faith fully formed by perfect love for God. This *fides caritate formata*, as it was known, or perfect love for God, rendered the individual "justifiable" on the basis of what "grace" had now accomplished in him or her. The net result was spiritually disastrous for at least two reasons:

(1) Who could ever claim that grace had worked in them a love for God so perfect that on that basis God could justify them as wholly righteous? Even in the Roman Catholic Church, the only people who can make such a claim are "the rarest of people worthy to be canonized as 'saints'" (in a quite different

---

6. *Works* 2:47. Italics original.

sense from the New Testament use of the term). And, yes, perhaps those to whom God gave a special revelation of Himself. But the net result of this plan of salvation was that very few could ever, in this life, enjoy the assurance of salvation. Indeed, as Cardinal Robert Bellarmine insisted, such assurance was the greatest of all Protestant heresies.[7]

(2) In keeping with this, grace was viewed virtually as a commodity to be dispensed by the church through its priests and sacraments. It might be resourced in Christ, but in itself it was something impersonal, a commodity—not the loving, caring, sacrificing, keeping, gracious Savior Himself.

Thus, Owen's great burden and emphasis in helping us to understand what it means to be a Christian is to say: Through the work of the Spirit, the heavenly Father gives you to Jesus and gives Jesus to you. You have Him. Everything you can ever lack is found in Him; all you will ever need is given to you in Him. "From his fullness we have all received, grace

---

7. Robert Bellarmine, *De Justificatione*, III.2.3, in *Disputationes de Controversiis Christianae Fidei adversus huius Temporaris Haerticos,* 4 vols. (Cologne, Germany: B. Gualterhus, 1619). It is worth noting here that in medieval theology, there was constant reference to "grace" and how justification is by grace. Technically, therefore, the church believed "by grace you have been saved through faith" (Eph. 2:5). But when they analyzed this carefully, the Reformers saw that justification took place on the basis of something accomplished in us that we had a share in producing. This was the justification of the ungodly *only when grace made him or her actually godly.* When this is not well understood, evangelical Christians who hear Roman Catholics speak about salvation and justification *by grace* are easily misled into thinking that Catholic theology has now become increasingly aligned with Reformation theology. But the truth, sadly, is that evangelical theology has become less and less aligned with the clarity of Reformation theology.

upon grace."[8] For the Father has "blessed us in Christ with every spiritual blessing in the heavenly places."[9] It is as true for the newest, weakest Christian as for the most mature believer: from the first moment of faith, we are fully, finally, irreversibly justified in Christ.

In this way, like Calvin before him, at a stroke Owen transforms our understanding of the nature of grace and salvation.[10] To explore fellowship with Christ, then, means that we need to explore both "the grace of our Lord Jesus Christ" with whom we have fellowship, and how it is that we have "fellowship" with Him in His grace.

For Owen, Christ's grace is multidimensional. It consists in His personal graciousness and attractiveness as the Mediator and Savior, in His favor and love toward us as sinners, and in His transforming us through the gift of His Spirit. Thus, to appreciate what it means to have fellowship with Him involves coming to understand how and why it is that He is able to save us. Here, Owen leads us to the very fountainhead of grace in the person of Christ. Christ is able to save us because He has united our human nature to His own divine nature in His one divine person as the Son of God.

We modern Christians are inclined to think of such language as this as belonging to the remote ivory tower world of

---

8. John 1:16. Notice that these words provide the ground for John's conclusion in 1:17, that "the law was given through Moses; grace and truth came through Jesus Christ."

9. Eph. 1:3.

10. See, for example, Calvin, *Institutes* 2.16.19 and 3.1.1.

ancient theology. In all likelihood, Owen would be disposed to tell us (rightly?) that we therefore know very little about either ancient theology or ancient theologians. This classical way of thinking about Christ was not developed in the security of academia but on the battlegrounds of gospel witness and church life, where thinking Christians were willing to suffer for the sake of rightly understanding and describing their beloved Savior. Owen belonged to their guild—where a passion to know and love Christ drove a desire to describe Him rightly in order to know and love Him more.

In this context, Owen well understood that unless Christ were truly and fully God and truly and fully man, He could not have been fitted or equipped to save us. This truth Owen saw embedded in the teaching of the New Testament, and nowhere more clearly than in the letter to the Hebrews. It was only as the God-man that the Lord Jesus "had room enough in his breast to receive, and power enough in his spirit to bear all the wrath that was prepared for us."[11]

Since all the fullness of God dwells in Him, and He received the Spirit without measure,[12] His bearing the judgment of God on the cross could not exhaust and destroy Him. Because He is so perfectly suited to our needs, therefore, Christ endears Himself to believers. He is just what we need, and He is all that we need:

---

11. *Works* 2:51.
12. Heb. 7:25; John 3:34.

There is no man that hath any want in reference unto the things of God, but Christ will be unto him that which he wants.

I speak of those who are given him of his Father. Is he *dead*? Christ is *life*. Is he *weak*? Christ is the *power* of God, and the *wisdom* of God. Hath he the *sense of guilt* upon him? Christ is complete *righteousness*. . . .

He hath a fitness to save, having pity and ability, tenderness and power, to carry on that work to the uttermost; and a fulness to save, of redemption and sanctification, or righteousness and the Spirit; and a suitableness to the wants of all our souls.[13]

From beginning to end, therefore, communion with Christ is all about *Christ*. When He fills the horizon of our vision, we find ourselves drawn to Him, embraced by Him, and beginning to enjoy Him.

COMMUNION WITH CHRIST IN PERSONAL GRACE

The New Testament's most frequent, and indeed most basic, description of the believer is that he or she is a person "in Christ." The expression and its variants overwhelmingly dominate the teaching of the Apostles. And one of the clues Scripture gives to help us understand what this means is to

---

13. *Works* 2:52.

express our union with Christ in terms of what Owen calls "conjugal relations," or, as we would say, "marriage." Through the ministry of the Spirit and by faith, we become united to Christ, "one" with Christ, in the way a man and a woman "become one flesh" in the marriage bond. This picture, already present in the Old Testament,[14] comes to fulfillment in the New in the relationship between Christ and His church. Christ rejoiced in this prospect in eternity, and He has made it a reality in time, enduring the humiliation, pain, and anguish of the cross. Christ, in all His saving grace and personal attractiveness, is offered to us in the gospel. The Father brings to His Son the bride He has prepared for Him, and asks both parties if they will have each other—the Savior if He will have sinners to be His; sinners if they will embrace the Lord Jesus as their Savior, Husband, and Friend.

Like many of his contemporaries, Owen saw this spiritual union and communion between Christ and the believer foreshadowed and described in the Old Testament book the Song of Solomon.[15] His exposition of the attractiveness of Christ to

---

14. Isa. 54:5; 61:10; 62:5; Ezek. 16:1–22; cf. the book of Hosea.

15. In his "Letter to the Reader" that prefaced James Durham's exposition of the Song, Owen wrote, "The more general persuasion of learned men is, that the whole is one holy declaration of that mystically spiritual communion, that is between the great Bridegroom and his Spouse, the Lord Christ and his church, and every believing soul that belongs thereunto" (James Durham, *Song of Solomon*, [repr. Edinburgh, Scotland: Banner of Truth Trust, 1997], p. 21). We find hints of a similar approach in Calvin. See *Institutes* 3.16.4, where he likens the Christian's rejection of a sinful lifestyle to Song of Solomon 5:3: "'I have washed my feet,' says the believing soul according to Solomon, 'how shall I defile them anew?'" Behind both Calvin and the Puritan tradition to which Owen belonged (with, among others, Richard Sibbes) lies the massive exposition of the Song of Solomon

the Christian is heavily influenced by the descriptions of the Lover and the expressions of affection of the Beloved. Though his analysis was typical for his day, few commentators today would follow him in the details of his exegesis.[16]

But what is paramount and striking in Owen's thinking is that being a Christian involves a deep *affection* for Christ. He is a person to be known, admired, and loved. Fellowship with Christ, therefore, involves a "mutual resignation" or self-giving between ourselves and Him. There is *"endless, bottomless, boundless grace* and compassion" in Christ, a "fulness of grace in the human nature of Christ"[17] of such proportions that, says Owen (in a stunning outburst of wonder and praise):

If all the world (if I may so say) set themselves to drink free grace, mercy, and pardon, drawing water continually from the wells of salvation; if they should set themselves to draw from one single promise, an angel standing by and crying, "Drink, O my friends, yea, drink abundantly, take so much grace and pardon as shall be abundantly sufficient for the world of sin which is in every one of you;"—They would not be able to sink the grace of the promise one hair's

by Bernard of Clairvaux (1090–1153), to which Calvin makes more frequent reference in other contexts.

16. I have treated Owen's exposition of Song of Solomon at greater length in *John Owen on the Christian Life* (Edinburgh, Scotland: Banner of Truth, 1987), pp. 78–86. It is of special interest and significance that his whole exposition of the Song is rooted in Revelation 3:20, which may well contain an allusion to Song 5:2.

17. *Works* 2:61. Italics original.

breadth. There is enough for millions of worlds, if they were; because it flows into it from an infinite, bottomless fountain.[18]

Thus, to become a Christian is, for Owen, to feel the weight of the Lord's words in Hosea 3:3 as if spoken personally to us: "You must dwell as mine for many days. You shall not play the whore, or belong to another man; so will I also be to you." In response, we yield our wills to Christ and to the way of salvation God has provided in Him, and say:

"Lord, I would have had thee and salvation in my way, that it might have been partly of mine endeavours, and as it were by the works of the law; I am now willing to receive thee and to be saved in thy way,—merely by grace: and though I would have walked according to my own mind, yet now I wholly give up myself to be ruled by thy Spirit; for in thee have I righteousness and strength, in thee am I justified and do glory;"— then doth it carry on communion with Christ as to the graces of his person. This it is to receive the Lord

---

18. *Works* 2:61–62. Owen penned this in 1657, some fifteen years after his *Display of Arminianism* and a decade after his landmark exposition of particular redemption, *The Death of Death in the Death of Christ*. It was his massive sense of the implications of Hebrews 7:25 ("he [Jesus] is able to save to the uttermost those who draw near to God through him, since he always lives to make intercession for them") that enabled Owen to see and feel the sufficiency of Christ for all who would come to Him. Thus he was able to issue a free, full, and unfettered summons to faith in Christ to all who listened to his preaching.

Jesus in his comeliness and eminency. Let believers exercise their hearts abundantly unto this thing. This is choice communion with the Son Jesus Christ.[19]

It is surely difficult for us to read passages like this—however quaint the language may seem at first—without feeling our hearts bursting as they seek to take in the sheer magnitude of what has happened to us in our coming to faith in such a Savior. We cannot spread our sin further than He can spread His grace. To meditate on this, to taste the waters of such a pure fountain, is surely to know "joy that is inexpressible and filled with glory."[20]

AFFECTIONATE COMMUNION

The reader of any work by John Owen is immediately struck by the sense of encountering an intellect of massive strength. All the more reason, therefore, to notice the emphasis he places on the role of the affections in the life of the Christian.

Owen and many of his contemporaries thought of human nature as a psychosomatic unity of body and soul; we have both physical and spiritual dimensions. Analyzing further how we function as human beings, they described the "spiritual" dimension in terms of mind, will, and affections.[21]

---

19. *Works* 2:58–59.

20. 1 Peter 1:9.

21. For a good discussion of how this relates to fallen humanity in Owen's theology, see

In this threefold distinction, we find an important clue to how Owen understands communion with Christ. It does indeed involve our *understanding* of who Christ is and what He has done; it also includes a *willingness* to give ourselves unreservedly to Him. But our communion with Him also enlivens and transforms the Christian's *affections*.

We are often (and rightly) reminded that we do not live the Christian life on the basis of our emotions, but we must never make the mistake of thinking that the gospel leaves our emotions untouched. Rather, it cleanses and transforms them by its power. We come to love what we formerly hated and to delight in what we formerly despised. Indeed, we experience what Owen calls "suitable consequential affections" toward Christ in light of His affectionate love for us.[22]

Christ delights in us. Owen delights to see the way this is expressed by Zephaniah:

> The LORD your God is in your midst,
> a mighty one who will save;
> he will rejoice over you with gladness;
> he will quiet you by his love;
> he will exult over you with loud singing.[23]

Stephen M. Griffiths, *Redeem the Time: The Problem of Sin in the Writings of John Owen* (Fearn, Ross-shire, Scotland: Christian Focus, 2001), pp. 57–93.

22. *Works* 2:117–18.
23. Zeph. 3:17.

Christ reveals His secrets to His people and thus transforms their relationship with Him from that of "servants" to "friends" because they know what their Master is doing.[24] How could He, who lays down His life for us, keep anything back from us that would be for our joy and lead to His pleasure and joy in us?

In turn, we find Christ becomes our delight. Even—or especially—in our weakness, His Spirit helps us.[25] He prays when we have no words to pray. Thus, one of the features of the spiritually minded believer is that his desires are greater than his words. By contrast, the person who does not delight in Christ will pray with words that far exceed his desires.

Before we were united to Christ, we could not delight in Him, because we were shut up under sin. But now, we delight in the new and living way that has been opened up for us to come to God through our Savior. We can now approach the throne of heaven with boldness. We are, Owen notes, like the Beloved in the Song of Solomon: "With great delight I sat in his shadow, and his fruit was sweet to my taste. He brought me to the banqueting house, and his banner over me was love."[26]

Owen is not slow to mention that such spiritual delight in Christ has a powerful moral effect on our lives. He writes, tellingly:

---

24. John 15:13–15.
25. Rom. 8:26–27.
26. Song 2:3b–4.

73

The line of *choicest communion*, is a line of the great-est *spiritual solicitousness*: *carelessness* in the enjoyment of Christ pretended, is a manifest evidence of a *false* heart."[27]

We have come to delight in Christ only when we have begun to live for Christ and a new sensitivity to and distaste for sin has been produced in us by His delight in us and ours in Him. This is how love functions:

When once the soul of a believer hath obtained sweet and real communion with Christ, it looks about him, watcheth all temptations, all ways whereby sin might approach to disturb him in his enjoyment of his dear Lord and Saviour, his rest and desire. How doth it charge itself not to omit anything, nor to do anything that may interrupt the communion obtained![28]

He adds, in vivid picture language that conjures up what "spiritual solicitousness" looks like in practice:

A believer that hath gotten Christ in his arms, is like one that hath found great spoils, or a pearl of price. He looks about him every way, and fears every thing that may deprive him of it.[29]

---

27. *Works* 2:126. Italics original.
28. *Works* 2:126.
29. Ibid.

Rather than producing carelessness, spiritual delight produces carefulness. It is because of this that the believer will place himself in a church context where all of the instruments of the Lord's blessings—worship, fellowship, the ministry of the Word, and the ordinances of baptism and the Lord's Supper—can be experienced. Christ blesses us in other ways and by other means, but only when we are walking in the ways and means He has prepared for us.

OUR WORTH IN HIS SIGHT

We live in a time when the "self-worth" and "self-image" of young people has become a major concern. Governments and institutions invest vast amounts of capital and human resources into dealing with the "problem." It should not surprise biblically instructed Christians that the results are in inverse proportion to the investment.

Telling young people that they are important—"You can become anything you want; you are our nation's future leaders," they are told—is clearly rhetoric designed to encourage a sense of self-worth. But the first statement is false. For instance, under normal circumstances, only one person can become president every four years. Since there is a lower age limit of thirty-five to becoming president, in the average life span, a maximum of eleven out of all of our contemporaries can achieve that office. The second statement leads to inevitable disappointment for many. For if all are leaders in the nation, who will follow? It need hardly be said that Christian parents can swallow this same secular mythology and assure their children that they (the parents) are preparing them for leadership. Scripture nowhere teaches us to do that. If anything, it teaches the reverse: we are training our children not for leadership but for service. If "leadership" (language almost entirely absent from the New Testament[30]) follows, well and good.

So, this modern self-worth mythology of some secular psychologists and educationalists—that we are all princesses and presidents in waiting—is doomed to failure.

Yet, precisely in this area, we find Owen, this colossus of seventeenth-century theology, in the midst of lengthy paragraphs of Latinate sentences, pointing us to the gospel answer to a contemporary epidemic. Our true worth is found in the value Christ has placed upon us, not in the valuation of our self-assessment. It is what He has done (and *who He is* as the One who has done it) that gives us real value and creates a sense of worth in us. For us, Christ was willing to become flesh; for us, He emptied Himself into human nature; for us, He became poor; for us, He was willing for His glory to be eclipsed. For us, He became a servant, drinking the cup of divine judgment and bearing the curse of God:

> 1. All that he parted withal, all that he did, all that he suffered, all that he doth as mediator; he parted withal, did, suffered, doth on the account *of his love*

---

30. The language that dominates the New Testament is that of serving and servanthood.

COMMUNION WITH THE SON

to and esteem of believers. He parted with the greatest glory, he underwent the greatest misery, he doth the greatest works that ever were, because he loves his spouse,—because he values believers. What can more, what can farther be spoken? how little is the depth of that which is spoken fathomed! how unable are we to look into the mysterious recesses of it! He so loves, so values his saints, as that, having from eternity undertaken to bring them to God, he rejoices his soul in the thoughts of it; and pursues his design through heaven and hell, life and death, by suffering and doing, in mercy and with power; and ceaseth not until he bring it to perfection. For,—

2. He doth so value them. As that he will not *lose* any of them to *eternity,* though all the world should combine to take them out of his hand.[31]

Here, we discover a Christ-valuation of ourselves that is calculated to dissolve all false self-worth and yet preserve us from pride. Christ's way of giving us worth has all the marks of divine genius. We exult in our privileges; He receives all the glory. We become royal children by His gift and grant, and so all self-valuation, for good or ill, is dissolved in His supreme valuation. And in turn, this—inevitably, surely—leads to the value we place on Christ and share with the psalmist: we have none in heaven beside Him and none on earth we desire like

---

31. *Works* 2:139. Italics original.

Him.[32] We value Him above all, and count everything as loss by comparison[33]:

> Christ and a dungeon, Christ and a cross, is infinitely sweeter than a crown, a scepter without him, to their souls . . . a despising of all things for Christ is the very first lesson of the gospel.[34]

Christ parted with everything for us; but He will never part with us. As a husband, He cares for us as His bride, as His own flesh. More than that,

> He is as a tender father, who, though perhaps he love his children alike, yet he will take most pains with, and give most of his presence unto, one that is sick and weak, though therein and thereby he may be made most forward, and, as it should seem, hardest to be borne with.[35]

Our response? Pressing home the marriage metaphor, Owen describes it as "the saints' chastity." In a disciplined way, we refuse to allow anything, in either our valuation of it or our affections toward it, to have a place that belongs only to Christ. We become sensitive to and love His indwelling Spirit

---

32. Ps. 73:25.
33. Phil. 3:8.
34. *Works* 2:137.
35. *Works* 2:141.

and do not grieve Him. We live out our lives on a pathway of worship and fellowship. We have received freely from Christ. In our delight in Him, we give ourselves freely, unreservedly, and joyfully back to Christ. This is communion indeed.

COMMUNION WITH CHRIST IN PURCHASED GRACE

Christ comes to us through His Spirit and draws us into communion with Himself. But, to borrow Calvin's fine expression, He comes to us "clothed with his gospel."[36] He is not a mystical Christ but an incarnate Christ. He is one and the same Lord and Christ who was conceived, born, baptized, tempted, suffered, died, was buried, rose, ascended, and now reigns at the right hand of His Father.

To speak of His "purchased grace," then, is simply to underline that our *koinōnia*, or fellowship, with Him implies that "there is almost nothing that Christ hath done, which is a spring of that grace whereof we speak, but we are said to do it with him."[37]

The privileges we enjoy, then, in Christ are shaped and determined by what He did as our representative and substitute. This Owen sees as three-dimensional: Christ's obedient life, His atoning death, and His ongoing intercession. Only as we view Christ (or "eye" Him, to use Owen's preferred

---

36. *Institutes* 3.2.6.
37. *Works* 2:155.

expression) in these ways do we come to appreciate how His work for us reshapes our lives.

In Scripture, obedience is a fundamental category for interpreting the work of Christ. It is implied in the fact that He is the *servant* of the Lord,[38] and His work is specifically described in terms of His obedience to His Father.[39] The holy Son assumed our frail flesh in the womb of the Virgin Mary, where it was sanctified by the Spirit from the beginning. His whole life was marked by a habit or disposition of obedience. More specifically, the Lord Jesus was actually obedient to the law of God—whether the law of nature that Adam was called to obey, or the law of Moses with all its distinctives governing the epoch from Moses to His own coming, or the specific law governing His work as Mediator.

In particular, although Owen thought that the terms *active* and *passive* used by theologians to analyze this obedience were improper, he resonated with what was intended by them. Christ was indeed always *active*, not passive, in enduring His sufferings (He was obedient to death). But His *active obedience*—his faithfulness and conformity to His Father's will throughout the whole course of His life—was not merely part of being the spotless lamb of God, without fault or sin, nor merely a necessary preamble to His real work for us. It was an *essential* part of that work. Christ must both *do* and *die* for us. For He must not only pay the price of death as the penalty for

---

38. Cf. Isa. 42:1, 19; Heb. 10:7.
39. Cf. Phil. 2:8; Heb. 5:8.

our sin, but also actually obtain life and righteousness for us by His life of obedience.

If Christ's obedience is limited to His death for us, then what He accomplished for us can only bring us back to the status of Adam before God on the day of his creation. It does not bring us forward to where Adam was called to be through a life of obedience. So Christ must *die*. But He must also *do*. Only then can He ground a full and final justification that includes both pardon for our sins through His death and our being counted fully and finally righteous through His life.

The glorious truth of the gospel—as Owen sees in the face of objections—is that participation in Christ in His obedience in both life and death means that we are as righteous as Christ Himself is before the judgment seat of God. While we have no righteousness of our own in which we can rest, the whole righteousness of Christ is ours since He obtained it for us and not for Himself. We are now as righteous before God as He is righteous, because it is only with His righteousness that we are righteous.

In terms of the colorful imagery of Zechariah 3:1–5, the filthy garments of our sin have been removed by the atoning death of Christ and the pure vestments He wove throughout His life, death, resurrection, and ascension have been placed upon us. Satan is rebuked and the child of God is secure in Christ.[40]

None of this, of course, minimizes the significance of Christ's death. As our High Priest, He gave Himself as a

---

40. *Works* 2:164.

sacrifice for our sins and satisfied the justice of God.[41] Our punishment became His; His freedom becomes ours. By His death, He paid the price of our redemption and thereby guaranteed our deliverance from the dominion of sin, Satan, and the world.[42]

Union with Christ in His death and resurrection means that we have died to sin and been raised into newness of life. Sin's dominion is broken, even though its presence and influence remains.[43]

For Owen, few things, if any, are more important for Christians to grasp than this. Every Christian pastor and counselor constantly encounters the same basic spiritual issues:

1. To convince those in whom sin evidently hath the dominion that such indeed is the case.

This, we might say, is the problem we face in *evangelism*.

2. To satisfy some that sin hath not the dominion over them, notwithstanding its restless acting itself in them

---

41. Throughout his ministry, Owen placed enormous emphasis on Christ's priestly ministry as belonging to the heart of the gospel. His *Vindiciae Evangelicae* (written in 1655 at the request of the Council of State in order to refute the teaching of the Socinians) contains a brief exposition of the significance of Christ's priestly ministry (*Works* 12:39); this was considerably enlarged in the 1674 publication of his *Exercitations on the Epistle to the Hebrews*, Part IV, "Concerning the Sacerdotal Office of Christ." See his *Exposition of the Epistle to the Hebrews*, 2:3–259. This is volume 19 in the twenty-four-volume set of Owen's *Works* as published by Johnstone and Hunter (Edinburgh, Scotland,1854–55). See also my introduction to John Owen, *The Priesthood of Christ* (Fearn, Ross-shire, Scotland: Christian Focus, 2012), pp. 13–23.

42. Eph. 2:1–3.

43. Rom. 6:1–14.

and warring against their souls; yet unless this can be done, it is impossible they should enjoy solid peace and comfort in this life.[44]

This is the perennial issue of *pastoral ministry*.

Owen finds the resolution of the latter in grasping what communion with Christ in His redemptive death and resurrection means. Christ died to the dominion of sin. Its reign was destroyed; it is no longer king over the believer. Once slaves of sin, we are now reborn as citizens in a new kingdom, members of a new family, the free servants of God, delivered by the ransom price of Christ's death "unto the hand of God."[45]

CHRIST CONTINUES AS A PRIEST FOREVER

But the priestly ministry of Christ belongs to the present as well as to the past. He died for our sins and was raised for our justification, "to carry on the complete work of purchased grace—, that is, by his intercession."[46] So He now appears in the presence of God for us,

> as it were to [re]mind him of the engagement made to him, for the redemption of sinners by his blood, and the making out the good things to them which

---

44. *Works* 7:517.
45. *Works* 2:166.
46. *Works* 2:168.

were procured thereby . . . he puts in his claim in our behalf.[47]

There is, Owen beautifully notes,

a life which he liveth for himself; namely, a life of inconceivable glory in his human nature. He led a mortal life in this world, a life obnoxious [vulnerable] unto misery and death, and died accordingly. This life is now changed into that of immortal, eternal glory. . . .

And not only so, but this life is his unto him the cause of, and is attended with, all that ineffable glory which he now enjoys in heaven. This life he lives for himself; it is his reward, the glory and honour that he is crowned withal. [48]

But since Christ made us His own in His covenant with His Father, and has united Himself to our flesh in His incarnation, death, and resurrection, we remain His. Owen, like Calvin before him, held that Christ sees His covenant bond with His people to be so strong that He regards them in some sense as one with Himself. Consequently, He considers Himself to be incomplete without us. And so He lives in heaven not only for Himself in glory, but for us in order to bring us there. The knowledge of this brings a sense of refreshment,

---

47. Ibid.
48. *Works* 22:534. Italics original.

joy, and thrill to believers now, just as it did to Stephen on the day of his death.[49]

This intercession lies at the heart of the church's faith.[50] It need not mean that Christ requires the use of words, but it does mean that He permanently appears before God in His priestly office "representing the efficacy of his oblation, accompanied with tender care, love and desires for the welfare, supply, deliverance and salvation of the church."[51] Owen argues that Christ's intercession, although it is not always recognized as such, is as essential for believers as His High Priestly sacrifice:

It is generally acknowledged that sinners could not be saved without the death of Christ; but that believers could not be saved without the life of Christ following it, is not so much considered. . . . But, alas! when all this was done, if he had only ascended into his own glory, to enjoy his majesty, honour, and dominion, without continuing his life and office in our behalf, we had been left poor and helpless; so that both we and all our right unto a heavenly inheritance should have been made a prey unto every subtle and powerful adversary.[52]

---

49. *Works* 22:535; see Acts 7:54–60.
50. Rom. 8:34; Heb. 4:15–16; 10:21–22; 1 John 2:1–2.
51. *Works* 22:541. Owen resolutely refuses to speculate further as to how Christ's intercession is exercised. For him, this is "the safest conception and apprehension that we can have of the intercession of Christ."
52. *Works* 22:542.

In a word, Christians find both stability and assurance in the application to themselves of our Lord's words: "I have prayed for you."

The chief blessing of this intercession is the gift of the Holy Spirit. Through Him, all that Christ has accomplished for us is revealed and applied to us. To that theme Owen will return.[53] But in the meantime, he bids us rest in this biblical truth: Christ "is able to save to the uttermost those who draw near to God through him, since he always lives to make intercession for them."[54] Those who enjoy communion with Him are reassured there is no lack in them that He cannot meet, no emptiness He cannot fill, no sin He cannot forgive, no enemy that can withstand the fact that the Christ who died for them lives forever for them at God's right hand. Having died to win our inheritance in the presence of God, He stands in that very presence to secure us for its full and final enjoyment. This is communion indeed.

THE PRIVILEGES OF COMMUNION WITH CHRIST

How do we come to enjoy communion with Christ, and what are the privileges and joys it brings to us?

Communion, in its very nature, is two sided. God's covenant relationship with His people, even when unilaterally established ("I will be your God") was always bilateral in its

---

53. See chapter 5 below.
54. Heb. 7:25.

realization ("you will be my people"). Something is required on both sides for covenant fellowship and communion to be enjoyed. The same is true of our *koinōnia* with the Lord Jesus.

Christ has already done everything that is required on His part: He has both kept the law for us and suffered for us in order to bring us absolution and righteousness. Now, through the gospel, He offers Himself to us as a Savior and Master, and promises the enlivening power of the Spirit to seal our union with Him.

Is anything then required on our part? Although Christ has paid the penalty for our sin, we are not actually pardoned and justified until we are united to Him. True, Christ has been absolved and justified as our representative, so that ultimately the Trinity should be glorified in our salvation and we ourselves come into a full enjoyment of it. But until we are "in Christ," His righteousness is not yet ours. We remain "by nature children of wrath."[55]

How, then, does this two-sided communion become a reality on both sides?

(1) Jesus Christ gives us His righteousness and removes our defilement. He provides us with:

  (a) A new acceptance with God: through the double imputation of our sin to Christ and His righteousness to us, guilt is removed and friendship is begun.

---

55. Eph. 2:3.

(b) A new acceptability before God: through the cleansing of the pollution of our hearts and the guilt of our past sin.

(2) Christians, in response, approve of the divine way of justification.

We, for our part, see first of all our need for receiving as a gift the righteousness before God that we lack in ourselves. We recognize that our own righteousness is of no value as a whole or in any part. We are hopelessly and helplessly undone, incapable of weaving for ourselves a garment of righteousness.

The gospel comes to us in our sense of spiritual bankruptcy to offer us another's righteousness in place of our own unrighteousness. Christ has obeyed in our place and died in our stead. We see in the cross the amazing power and wisdom of God. He has devised a plan that preserves His absolute justice, demonstrates His love, and brings Him glory, yet simultaneously deals with our guilt and brings us salvation. The cross becomes to us "the trysting place where heaven's love and heaven's justice meet."[56] We now also sing:

Upon a life I did not live,
Upon a death I did not die;
Another's life, another's death,
I stake my whole eternity.[57]

---

56. From the hymn "Beneath the Cross of Jesus" by Elizabeth C.D. Clephane (1830–69).

57. From the hymn "Upon a Life I Did Not Live" by Horatius Bonar (1808–89).

Owen leads us to see in the cross such a demonstration of the love of God that Paul was required to ransack the vocabulary of love to describe its wonder:

> Here [in Titus 3:4–7] is use made of every word almost, whereby the exceeding rich grace, kindness, mercy, and goodness of God may be expressed, all concurring in this work. . . . goodness, benignity, readiness to communicate of himself and his good things that may be profitable to us. . . . Mercy, love, and propensity of mind to help, assist, relieve. . . . Mercy, forgiveness, compassion, tenderness to them that suffer, . . . free pardoning bounty, undeserved love.[58]

Grasp this and joy breaks forth in the heart. Here at last is peace and security with God. Owen waxes eloquent with language that surely expresses the wonder of his own experience in discovering the power of the truth of the gospel. Now believers

> remember what was their state and condition while they went about to set up a righteousness of their own, and were not subject to the righteousness of Christ,— how miserably they were tossed up and down with conflicting thoughts. Sometimes they had hope, and sometimes were full of fear; sometimes they thought themselves in some good condition, and anon were at

---

58. *Works* 2:190.

the very brink of hell, their consciences being racked and torn with sin and fear: but now "being justified by faith, they have peace with God," Rom. v. 1. All is *quiet and serene*; not only that *storm* is over, but they are in the *haven* where they would be. They have abiding peace with God.[59]

Knowing the story of Owen's own spiritual pilgrimage, and the significance for him of the story of Christ stilling the storm, these words are doubly impressive. He knew whereof he spoke. He remembered "the wormwood and the gall." He had been in the boat; he had cried out. The Savior had brought him peace at last. The storm was over.

But something else characterizes real communion in Christ's righteousness. We bless God not only because of the effect of Christ's righteousness on us but also because Christ's gaining it for us is the divinely planned means of exalting and honoring Him. In the very embracing of Christ for ourselves, we realize that the Savior is found to be great and glorious in Himself, honored by His Father with the name above all names, adored by angels and worshiped by saints both on earth and in heaven.[60] And through Him, God the blessed Trinity, in each of His three persons, is "exceedingly glorified in the pardon, justification, and acceptance of poor sinners."[61]

---

59. Ibid. Italics original.
60. Phil. 2:5–11; Rev. 5:8–14.
61. *Works* 2:193.

THE GREAT EXCHANGE

So the great exchange, or *commutation*, takes place—we take what is Christ's and He takes what is ours—Christ's righteousness for our sinfulness. In our sin, guilt, and shame, He summons us to come to Him:

> Why? What to do? "Why, this is mine," saith Christ; "this agreement I made with my Father, that I should come, and take thy sins, and bear them away: they were my lot. Give me thy *burden*, give me all thy *sins*. Thou knowest not what to do with them; I know how to dispose of them well enough, so that God shall be glorified and thy soul delivered."[62]

Thus we see that Christ really has taken our place. In our place, He has answered all the claims against us of the law we have broken. And in response, we receive Him by faith. We lay our sin on His shoulders on the cross, giving it up entirely to Him. And though we do this in a once-for-all sense in coming to Him, this becomes the ongoing daily rhythm of our lives.

What we need to grasp is that nothing could more delight the Lord Jesus than that we should give our sins and ourselves to Him. This *honors* Him as our Savior; not to do so would be to dishonor Him. In turn, when we experience this, we see His true worth at last. The result?

---

62. *Works* 2:194. Italics original.

Who would not love him? "I have been with the Lord Jesus," may the poor soul say: "I have left my sins, my burden, with him; and he hath given me his righteousness, wherewith I am going with boldness to God. I was *dead*, and am *alive*; for he *died* for me: I was *cursed,* and am *blessed;* for he was made a *curse for me*: I was *troubled*, but have *peace*; for the *chastisement of my peace* was upon him. I knew not what to do, nor whither to cause *my sorrow* to go; by him have I received *joy unspeakable and glorious*. If I do not love him, delight in him, obey him, live to him, die for him, I am worse than the devils in hell."[63]

This is to give Christ, who has preeminence over all things, the preeminence in our hearts, so that, as Owen vividly puts it, He is no longer "jostled up and down among other things."[64]

As we meditate on this, now from the perspective of our own sinfulness, and then from the perspective of Christ's saving grace, we will more and more come to enjoy the fullness of His love in ongoing communion with Him.

THE HABIT OF GRACE

Christ sends His Holy Spirit to His people in keeping with His promise that the Spirit who was with the disciples in the

---

63. *Works* 2:195. Italics original.
64. *Works* 2:196.

person of the Lord Jesus would come to indwell and transform them. The Father in due course put the Spirit "into the hand of Christ for us."[65] The result is that we are renewed and subsequently begin to produce the fruit of the Spirit. The "habit of grace" is produced in us, that is, "a new, gracious, spiritual life, or principle, created, and bestowed on the soul, whereby it is changed in all its faculties and affections, fitted and enabled to go forth in the way of obedience unto every divine object that is proposed unto it, according to the mind of God."[66]

This "habitual grace" is not to be identified with the indwelling Spirit Himself, but is produced by His ministry in us. It is rather the creation by Christ and through the Spirit of a new disposition in the believer. For that reason, we need to think of it as a gift of Christ purchased at the high cost of His death, and thus to value it. We then come to see the Lord Jesus as "the great Joseph, that hath the disposal of all the granaries of the kingdom of heaven committed unto him."[67]

We also come to see Christ as our Savior, who, having shed His precious blood for us, now sprinkles us with it to cleanse us. For in His grace, Christ not only pardons past sins but also sanctifies our present imperfect works. This enhances our delight in the new relationship we enjoy with the Father in and through His Son. For the Father sees us and all we do

---

65. *Works* 2:199.
66. *Works* 2:200.
67. *Works* 2:203.

through the lens of our union and fellowship with Christ. He not only *covers* our bad works; He *adorns* our good works. This is grace indeed, and delivers us from that inherent suspicion of God that Owen seems to have frequently encountered in his ministry. Rather than hiding His grace-gift in the sand out of fear and paralysis because of our sinful hearts, we discover that—like the loving Father He is—He is pleased with the lives and deeds of His children, imperfect though they are: "So that the saints' good works shall meet them one day with a changed countenance, that they shall scarce know them: that which seemed to them to be black, deformed, defiled, shall appear beautiful and glorious; they shall not be afraid of them, but rejoice to see and follow them."[68]

Christ also cleanses us inwardly. We are washed and sanctified in Him.[69] In addition, a new principle dominates our lives. In what Thomas Chalmers would later call "the expulsive power of a new affection,"[70] our lives become characterized by opposition to our sin as we rest in Christ and grace dwells and works in us: "In the understanding, it is light; in the will, obedience; in the affections, love; in all, faith."[71]

Yet this communion is by no means static. It is a communion enjoyed through faith. Without Christ, we can do

---

68. *Works* 2:171.

69. 1 Cor. 1:30; Titus 3:6.

70. The title of his most famous sermon. Thomas Chalmers (1780–1847) was one of the most impressive Christian thinkers of the nineteenth century and the leader of the 1843 Disruption in the Church of Scotland.

71. *Works* 2:172.

nothing.[72] Every new act of obedience involves a new experience of Christ's grace.

ADOPTION—OUR HIGHEST PRIVILEGE

To contemplate all the privileges of communion with Christ would be, Owen says, "work for a man's whole life."[73] Yet these are all summed up in what he regards as "the head, the spring, and fountain whence they all arise and flow."[74] This—the highest privilege of all—is adoption into the family of God with all the rights and privileges of knowing Him as our heavenly Father.

Outside of Christ, we were strangers to the family of God both on earth and in heaven. But now we are brought near and made heirs. In Christ the Son, we have become the adopted sons of God: "Adoption is the authoritative translation of a believer, by Jesus Christ, from the family of the world and Satan, into the family of God, with his investiture in all the privileges and advantages of that family."[75] Thus, we enter into the manifold privileges that belong to the royal children of the heavenly King.

At first glance, it may seem strange that Owen discusses the theme of adoption within the context of communion with the

---

72. John 15:5.
73. *Works* 2:207.
74. Ibid.
75. Ibid.

Son. Adoption, after all, is by definition an act of the Father, and its confirmation is effected by the Spirit in His capacity as the "Spirit of sonship." But Owen's reasoning is fairly obvious: in union and communion with Christ, we become joint heirs with Him. So while each of the divine persons plays His particular role in adoption, it is appropriate to discuss adoption as the highest privilege of our union with Christ.

But in what do we enjoy communion as adopted children? Owen gives a fourfold answer:

(1) We enjoy the liberty of the children of God. We are set free from the hold of the old family. No longer is its influence dominant—even if we are not entirely free from its atmosphere and even its menacing influence. There is all the difference in the world between obeying the Father who has given His Son for us, so that we can be sure He will also give us everything we need, and being in bondage to the law while making our best efforts to keep it.

(2) We have a new title, and as royal sons enjoy "a feast of fat things,"[76] not least in the church, where we have the privilege of belonging to the family of God and being served by, and in turn loving and serving, its members. More than that, there is a sense in which the whole world is ours to enjoy, because it belongs to and is preserved by our Father. No child in this family can ever justly complain that his Father has set up a

76. *Works* 2:216.

restrictive regime without pleasures and joy. Isaac Watts was surely reflecting on this when he wrote:

> The men of grace have found,
> Glory begun below.
> Celestial fruits on earthly ground
> From faith and hope may grow.
> The Hill of Zion yields
> A thousand sacred sweets
> Before we reach the heav'nly ground,
> Or walk the golden streets.[77]

(3) We experience boldness before the face of God. In Christ, we are as righteous as He is before God. We have the privilege of calling Him "Abba, Father." We can ask anything in Jesus' name. What more could we ask for?

(4) We experience affliction. But for the child of God, affliction is always chastisement—the action of the Father. This, as Owen rightly points out, is precisely the burden of Hebrews 12:5–11. It is one of the chief distinctions between Christians and unbelievers. The latter seek but do not find any ultimate meaning in their suffering; as a result, unbelievers must attempt to *create* meaning. But not so Christians. For Scripture teaches them that, in Christ, trials have a goal. God is treating His people as sons by training them. Were He indifferent to us

---

77. From the hymn "Come We That Love the Lord" by Isaac Watts (1674–1748).

in our sin and waywardness, questions could rightly be raised about our legitimacy. In this sense, all discipline is evidence of His love. More than that, suffering in the Christian life is the training ground of the soul. The Father is equipping His children through adversity. If our earthly fathers discipline us for our good, how much more will the heavenly Father, who knows His children through and through?

Thus, when we were united to Christ, a transaction and transition of monumental proportions took place. It would be a tragedy if we did not catch a glimpse of the grandeur of what this means—it is nothing less than union and communion with the Son of God in our flesh.

John Owen was deeply impressed by the sheer magnitude of God's grace. He marveled at the way in which all of the blessings the Father grants actually come to us only, but fully, through our union and communion with Christ.

For this reason, it is not surprising that Owen paid so much attention to what it means to be "found in Christ" and through Him enjoy communion with God. Having reflected on this central dimension of Owen's thinking, we must now explore how he understands what it means to enjoy communion in and with the third person of the Godhead, the Holy Spirit.

CHAPTER FIVE

Communion
with the Holy Spirit

It is unnecessary to say that he is the prince of divines. To master his works is to be a profound theologian. Owen is said to be prolix, but it would be truer to say that he is condensed. His style is heavy because he gives notes of what he might have said, and passes on without fully developing the great thoughts of his capacious mind. He requires hard study, and none of us ought to grudge it.[1]

—CHARLES HADDON SPURGEON

A century ago, B.B. Warfield described John Calvin as "the theologian of the Holy Spirit."[2] It was as wise an insight as it was unexpected. For among his many contributions to

---

1. Charles Haddon Spurgeon, *Commenting and Commentaries* (London: Passmore and Alabaster, 1876), p. 103.

2. B.B. Warfield, *Calvin as a Theologian and Calvinism Today* (Philadelphia: Presbyterian Board of Publication, 1909; repr. London: Evangelical Press, n.d.), p. 5. I. John Hesselink notes a predecessor in Charles Lelièvre in 1901, but dates Warfield's comment by the publication of his collected writings. See *The Calvin Handbook*, ed. H.J. Selderhuis (Grand Rapids, Mich.: Eerdmans, 2009), p. 299.

the Christian church, Calvin systematically demonstrated that the Spirit is the One through whom all the blessings of God, planned by the Father and purchased by the Son, become ours.

The reason Warfield had few predecessors who saw Calvin this way was in part because Calvin neither wrote a separate treatise on the Holy Spirit nor treated His person and work as a distinct focus in his *Institutes of the Christian Religion*. Thus, the task of focused and extended exposition of the Spirit's ministry awaited another.

Into this doctrinal gap in the literature of the church, John Owen willingly stepped. He consciously (and rightly) saw his *Discourse on the Holy Spirit*[3] as one of his major contributions to the history of theology. In his introductory comments to his exposition, he wrote, "I know not any who ever went before me in this design of representing the whole economy of the Holy Spirit, with all his adjuncts, operations, and effects."[4]

THE FORGOTTEN PERSON

Fifty years ago, in the context of what came to be called "the charismatic movement," the Holy Spirit was frequently described as "the forgotten person of the Godhead." Sometimes the statement reflected more on its authors than it did on the story of the church. One could hardly be really familiar with the lives and writings of the Reformers, the Puritans, and

3. See volumes 3 and 4 of the Goold edition of his *Works*.
4. *Works* 3:7.

the great figures of the First and Second Great Awakenings while accusing them of forgetting the Spirit.

In fact, what was usually meant was not that the Spirit *Himself* had been forgotten or ignored, but that the particular gifts of tongues, working of miracles, and prophecy, all of which were present in the New Testament church, had been forgotten. But even this was not a true or fair assessment. For the church fathers, Reformers, and mainstream figures of the Great Awakenings were convinced from Scripture that—as elsewhere in redemptive history—these unusual gifts were given as confirmatory signs of new revelation. Unlike the Spirit's powerful work of regeneration (on which they had much to say), these gifts, they believed, were never intended to be permanent features of the church's life.[5]

One aspect of the shift of emphasis that appeared in evangelicalism in the 1960s was the separation in many contexts of the gifts of the Spirit from the person of the Spirit, and more generally the gifts of Christ from the knowledge of Christ. Hand in hand with this—as the moral downfall of not a few made clear—was the confusion of gifts with graces, mistaking the exercise of unusual "powers" for walking in the Spirit. What was particularly striking in the teaching, preaching, and writing on spiritual gifts was the way in which the biblical narrative of the Spirit's ministry was ignored—especially His relationship to the Lord Jesus Christ.

---

5. I have discussed this in greater detail in *The Holy Spirit* (Downers Grove, Ill.: Inter-Varsity Press, 1996), pp. 207–38.

Against this background, John Owen's grand-scale exposition of the person and work of the Spirit breathes a different air. Axiomatic for Owen is that if we are to experience the power of the Spirit in our lives, and the wonder of the new creation, we must first become familiar with His ministry in the life of the Savior Himself.

Our communion with the Spirit is dependent on, and shaped by, His communion with Christ and Christ's with Him. For, as we shall see Owen stress, the Spirit who comes upon believers is one and the same Spirit who dwelt on the Lord Jesus. He received the Spirit to engage in His ministry as Redeemer; He has now given this very same Spirit to all who are united to Him by faith.

So, our first step toward appreciating what it means to enjoy the communion of the Holy Spirit is to trace His presence in the ministry of Jesus.

CHRIST AND THE SPIRIT

Owen frequently refers to the words of Psalm 45:7 as descriptive of Jesus' communion with the Spirit: "You have loved righteousness and hated wickedness. Therefore God, your God, has anointed you with the oil of gladness beyond your companions." These words, applied to Christ in Hebrews 1:9, find their fulfilment in the way in which He received the Spirit without measure.[6]

---

6. John 3:34.

Jesus, who gives us the Spirit, is the One upon whom the Spirit came. He received, bore, and was borne by the Spirit throughout His life and ministry, not only *prior to* our receiving Him but also *with a specific view to* our receiving Him as the Spirit of Christ. Thus, the Spirit who was present in and through the life of Jesus is the very same Spirit who is now given to all believers.

There are not two Holy Spirits. The One through whom the Savior was conceived in the womb of the virgin is the One who conceives us spiritually when we are "born of the Spirit."[7] This is none other than the One who empowered the Savior throughout His ministry from womb to cross, from tomb to throne. Christ received the Spirit, was filled with the Spirit, and walked in the Spirit in order that on His ascension He might give the Spirit who dwelt on Him to all who believe in Him.[8] Only the Spirit of Christ has the capacity to transform us to be like Christ.[9]

For Owen, then, there are several stages in our Lord's relationship to the Holy Spirit in connection with His ministry to Him as the Messiah.[10] In fact, Owen walks his readers through ten specific works of the Spirit on Jesus.[11] These can be summarized in four ways:

---

7. John 3:3, 6, 8.

8. Acts 2:33.

9. 2 Cor. 3:18.

10. Owen wonderfully expounds this in two chapters of his *Pneumatologia; or, A Discourse Concerning the Holy Spirit*, book 2, chapters 3–4. *Works* 3:159–88.

11. *Works* 3:162–83.

(1) The incarnation of Christ. The conception of Jesus has all the characteristic marks of the Spirit's work. As the Spirit over-shadowed the darkness in the first work of creation, so also He overshadowed the darkness of the womb of the Virgin Mary. In the conception of the Savior, grace and nature were joined together in perfect and holy harmony.

(2) The ministry of Christ. For Owen, it was axiomatic that although our Lord lived in the power of the Spirit, He "acted grace as a man." Everything He accomplished for us He did as the divine Son of God, but did so as a man—fully man, truly man. He shared every aspect of our human condition, apart from sin. And He did so resting in the presence, communion, and power of the Holy Spirit.

This is seen in two ways:

(a) In His human nature, Jesus "grew"—not from sin to holiness as such, but *in holiness*, from holiness to holiness. He was not a "freak" or a "superboy." The Spirit enabled Him to make progress step by step with His natural maturing. This is implied by Luke when he says that Jesus grew in wisdom as well as stature and in favor with God as well as with man.[12]

There was nothing *non*human, *a*human, or *super*human about the obedience of Jesus. His understanding—under the influence of the Holy Spirit—developed in harmony with His mental capacities: "In the representation, then, of things anew

_____

12. Luke 2:52.

to the human nature of Christ, the wisdom and knowledge of his human nature was *objectively* increased, and in new trials and temptations he *experimentally* learned the new exercise of grace. And this was the constant work of the Holy Spirit on the human nature of Christ."[13]

The Messiah did not come immediately from heaven to the cross. Rather, Jesus grew. The fruit of the Spirit in His life went hand-in-glove with the natural development of all His individual human characteristics. But this "natural development" was the fruit of His submission to the work of the Spirit. Therein lay the intimacy and the beauty of His experience of the love of His Father through His communion with the Spirit: "He dwelt in him in fullness; for he received not him by measure. And continually, upon all occasions, he gave out of his unsearchable treasures grace for exercise in all duties and instances of it. From hence was he habitually holy, and from hence did he exercise holiness entirely and universally in all things."[14]

(b) At His baptism, according to Owen, Jesus entered into the fullness of the Spirit, not for progress in holiness, but for the fulfilment of His messianic ministry. Gifts were given to Him by the Spirit to equip Him for the climactic stages of the ages-old conflict between the kingdom of God and the powers of darkness. Sustained by God's Word ("the sword of the Spirit"), He simultaneously obeyed His Father, worked miracles, maintained His integrity, and caused Satan to flee.

---

13. *Works* 3:170. Italics original.
14. *Works* 3:170–71.

(3) The cross of Christ. Owen understood Hebrews 9:13–14 as referring to the Spirit's sustaining of the Lord Jesus in His sacrificial death. It was "through the eternal Spirit" that our Lord "offered himself without blemish to God."[15] Only through His communion with the Holy Spirit could Jesus bear the weight of the sins of the world and make atonement for them.

(a) The Spirit supported Jesus in His decision to offer Himself to the Father throughout the whole course of His life, with a view to His sacrificial death.

(b) He sustained Jesus as He came near to the gate of the temple when, in the garden of Gethsemane, He caught sight at close range of the bloody altar that awaited Him.

(c) He undergirded Jesus in the breaking of His heart and the engulfing of His soul as He experienced the dereliction of Calvary.

(d) Owen adds a further moving touch to help us grasp the wonder of the communion of the Son with the Spirit. If, on the cross, our Lord Jesus Christ committed His spirit into the hands of His Father, to what did He commit His body? *Externally*, Owen says, it was guarded by the holy angels, mounting watch over the garden tomb. But *internally*, the Spirit preserved it from physical corruption in the darkness of the tomb, just as He had preserved it from moral corruption

---

15. *Works* 3:176.

in the darkness of the virgin's womb. From womb to tomb, the Son was always in communion with the Spirit.

(4) The exaltation. The Father exalted His Son by His resurrection and ascension. Yet the New Testament also teaches that the Son has power to lay down His life and to take it up again. Father and Son are together harmoniously active in the exaltation of the resurrection. But Owen also notes the role of the Holy Spirit in the resurrection-exaltation.[16] The Spirit declared Him to be Son of God with power through the resurrection; the Spirit vindicates Him in the resurrection. This is a work of transformation, and its end result is His glorification. As Owen puts it, "He who first made his nature holy, now made it glorious."[17] Not only then from womb to tomb, then, but from womb to glory, the Spirit was the companion of the Savior.

What is the significance of this? It is that the Spirit cannot rightly be known (and therefore communion with Him cannot be fully enjoyed) apart from Christ—just as Christ cannot be known apart from the Spirit. For the identity in which we have communion with the Spirit is defined for us by His intimate relationship to the incarnate Savior. He is the Spirit of Christ. He is intimately knowledgeable about Christ. He takes what is Christ's and gives it to us with the goal of transforming us into Christ's likeness.[18]

---

16. Rom. 1:4.
17. *Works* 3:183.
18. John 16:13–15.

Christ Gives His Spirit

In the Upper Room, Jesus had promised the Apostles that He would ask the Father for the privilege of sending the Spirit to the church.[19] In the sending of the Spirit, both Father and Son are active.[20] Indeed, all three persons are engaged, since the Spirit who is *sent* also *comes*. In this sense, the Spirit comes from both the Father and the Son, and this "business of sending the Holy Ghost by Christ," Owen says, "argues his personal procession also from him, the Son."[21] This, of course, is the Augustinian doctrine of the *double procession* of the Spirit. It is the clue to the nature of the eternal relationship within the being of God between the Spirit and the Son. Granted, there is great mystery here; it is also true for Owen that the fact that Father and Son together send the Spirit is an indication of the Spirit's relation to them both in the inner life of God as well as in His external activity toward the world.

Thus, within the life of God the Trinity, the Spirit proceeds from both Father and Son to one another. Just as He is the bond of union between the Father and Son and believers, so He is the bond of union between the Father and Son.[22]

The Spirit is given to us in light of Christ's costly obedience; we receive Him freely as a gift in which we rejoice. In

---

19. John 14:6.
20. John 14:16, 26; 15:26.
21. *Works* 2:226.
22. John 17:20–23.

COMMUNION WITH THE HOLY SPIRIT

Owenian terms, we "eye" Him, ask for Him, receive Him, and admire Him. We "eye" Him in the sense of setting mind and heart on what Scripture teaches us about Him, and seeking by faith to grasp all that He is to us.

RECEIVING THE SPIRIT

But what does it mean to receive the Spirit of Christ? As we do so in faith, the Spirit comes to indwell us personally. This lies at the heart of the new covenant promise. But what is it about this covenant that is so *new*? Here are Owen's words:

> Our union with Christ consists in this, the same Spirit dwelling in him and us.[23]

> We therefore partake of the very same juice and fatness with the root and tree, being nourished thereby.[24]

Thus, the very life that is in the tree is also in the branches. This mind-stretching and life-transforming truth is grasped only when the Spirit comes to open our eyes to the truth of God's Word. We should never separate our need of the Spirit from our possession of the Word, or vice-versa. The first would be the error of the rationalist and the second of the mystic. The Spirit comes to open the eyes of our understanding to the

23. *Works* 11:337. Cf. 11:338.
24. *Works* 11:340.

revelation God has given us, not to give each individual new revelation. Rather, He comes to lead us into the embrace of the truth already revealed. To be "led" by the Spirit, therefore, in biblical terms, involves embracing and obeying the revelation God has given to all, not following private revelation given to individuals.[25]

The immediate fruit of the Spirit's coming to us is the bond of our union with Christ.[26] From this union flows all our communion with Him. As He comes to indwell us, He enlivens us, leads us, supports and strengthens us, and produces in us Christlike character and qualities. He both restrains us from sin and sanctifies us more and more.

COMMUNION WITH THE HOLY SPIRIT

In His Farewell Discourses, Jesus said that it was to the advantage of His disciples that He was leaving them[27]; in His place, the Spirit would come. He comes to us shaped, as it were, by Christ's communion with Him. He is "another Helper" (i.e. in addition to, in place of, and of the same character as Jesus Himself). He ministers to us as the vicar of Christ. His presence in our lives is the great "relic" that the Lord Jesus has left

---

25. Thus, in parallel contexts, to be filled with the Spirit (Eph. 5:18) and to "let the word of Christ dwell in you richly" (Col. 3:16) are two sides of the same reality.

26. A rich exposition of this union is found, like gold hidden in the hills, in Owen's massive *Doctrine of the Saints' Perseverance*, in *Works* 11:336ff.

27. John 16:7.

to the church. Virtually everything in the Christian life flows from and depends on this.

What, then, is the nature of the Spirit's ministry? There are, according to Owen, four ways in which the Spirit evidences His presence and power in communion with the believer: indwelling, unction, earnest, and seal. Since, for all practical purposes, Owen regards the Spirit's presence as both unction and earnest as aspects of His indwelling, we can reduce this to two: His indwelling and His sealing.

The Spirit indwells every believer mysteriously. But He does so, Owen emphasizes, personally, as the Spirit of Christ. Owen makes a distinction, which he shares with other Puritan writers on this theme, between the indwelling of the Holy Spirit as the Spirit of holiness and His self-manifestation as Comforter. The former is a constant ministry. The Spirit is always, under all circumstances, at all times, making us holy. He uses every situation—joys, trials, successes, and failures—to conform us to the image of God's Son.

But the *manifestations* of the Spirit as Comforter, Owen argues, are intermittent. He does not always bring us a conscious sense of the comforts of the gospel. This is an important point for the simple reason that Owen believes we need to distinguish between the indwelling of the Spirit (a constant) and the manner in which He manifests that identity in and to the consciousness of the individual believer (a variable). One expression of this is seen in the variations among believers in their experience of assurance; they not only differ from each other, but they may differ from themselves from one week to another.

Nevertheless, Owen holds that the indwelling of the Holy Spirit brings with it several distinct blessings.

(1) The Spirit comes to give the believer direction and guidance. This guidance is always moral and *extrinsic*, in the sense that the Spirit gives it to us objectively in the Word He has inspired. But it is *intrinsic* in the sense that it is also internal and efficient. The Holy Spirit illumines our understanding of the Scriptures and enables us to embrace their truth.

This is tantamount to what the Apostle John means when it speaks of believers receiving the anointing of the Spirit[28] and therefore not needing anyone to teach them. Clearly, in another sense, John believes Christians need to be taught (he himself is in the act of teaching them by his letter). Rather, what he has in view is that the Spirit has revealed Christ to them.

(2) The Spirit also comes to give support; He helps us in our infirmities.[29]

(3) Equally significant, the Spirit comes to exercise an ongoing internal restraint on our lives, to prevent us running headlong into sin. More than that, He injects into our obedience a spirit

---

28. 1 John 2:20, 27.
29. Rom. 8:26.

of joy and gladness that banishes our native sluggishness. Peter is his paradigm here: "Peter was broken loose and running down hill apace, denying and forswearing his Master; Christ puts a restraint upon his spirit by a look towards him."[30]

This, in turn, becomes for Owen a paradigm of the work of the Holy Spirit, who inwardly "drops an awe" upon our spirits[31] that causes this holy restraint in order that we may not fall into sin.

DISTINGUISHING THE SPIRIT FROM THE SERPENT

Against this background, Owen raises an important question: How do we distinguish the promptings of the Spirit of grace in His guiding and governing of our lives from the delusions of the spirit of the world and of our own sinful heart? This is a hugely important question if we are to be calm and confident that the spirit with whom we are communing really is the *Holy* Spirit.

Owen suggests four ways in which the Spirit and the serpent are to be distinguished[32]:

(1) The leading of the Spirit, he says, is regular, that is, according to the *regulum*: the rule of Scripture. The Spirit does not work in us to give us a new rule of life, but to help us

---

30. *Works* 11:349.
31. Ibid.
32. *Works* 11:363–65.

understand and apply the rule contained in Scripture. Thus, the fundamental question to ask about any guidance will be: Is this course of action consistent with the Word of God?

(2) The commands of the Spirit are not grievous. They are in harmony with the Word, and the Word is in harmony with the believer as new creation. The Christian believer consciously submitted to the Word will find pleasure in obeying that Word, even if the Lord's way for us is marked by struggle, pain, and sorrow. Christ's yoke fits well; His burden never crushes the spirit.[33]

(3) The "motions" of the Spirit are orderly. Just as God's covenant is ordered in all things and secure,[34] so the promised gift of that covenant, the indwelling Spirit, is orderly in the way in which He deals with us. Restlessness is not a mark of communion with the Spirit but of the activity of the evil one. Perhaps Owen had particular members of his congregations in mind when he wrote:

> We see some poor souls to be in such bondage as to be hurried up and down, in the matter of duties at the pleasure of Satan. They must run from one to another, and commonly neglect that which they should do. When they are at prayer, then they should

---

33. Matt. 11:28–30.
34. 2 Sam. 23:5.

be at the work of their calling; and when they are at their calling, they are tempted for not laying all aside and running to prayer. Believers know that this is not from the Spirit of God, which makes "every thing beautiful in its season."[35]

(4) The "motions," or promptings of the Spirit, Owen says, always tend to glorify God according to His Word. He brings Jesus' teaching into our memories; He glorifies the Savior; He pours into our hearts a profound sense of the love of God for us.

How, then, does the Spirit act on the believer? The Spirit comes to us as an earnest, a pledge, a down payment on final redemption. He is here and now the foretaste of future glory. But His presence is also an indication of the incompleteness of our present spiritual experience.

Owen here writes in sharp contrast to those who spoke of release from the influence of indwelling sin and struggle through the liberty of the Spirit. Precisely because He is the firstfruits and not yet the final harvest, there is a sense in which the indwelling of the Spirit is the cause of the believer's groaning: "We ourselves who have the firstfruits of the Spirit groan inwardly as we wait eagerly for our adoption as sons, the redemption of our bodies."[36] The presence of the Spirit brings us already a foretaste of future glory, but also, simultaneously, creates within us a sense of the incompleteness of our present spiritual experience.

---

35. *Works* 11:364.
36. Rom. 8:23.

This, for Owen, is how communion with the Spirit—understood biblically—brings joy into the life of the believer and yet a deep sense that the fullness of joy is not yet.

SEALED WITH THE SPIRIT

The Spirit who comes to indwell also comes as a seal. Owen was intensely interested in what Scripture means when it speaks about believers being sealed by the Spirit.[37] As late as 1667, he wrote: "I am not very clear on the certain particular intendment of this metaphor."[38] At that time, he reasoned that it is *promises*, not *persons*, that are in view in this sealing. He concluded that we are sealed when we enjoy a fresh sense of the love of God within us and a comfortable persuasion of acceptance with God. The promises of God—the promises of grace in salvation—are sealed to us and we, correspondingly, enter into the enjoyment of Him.

However, in his work on the Holy Spirit as Comforter,[39] Owen wrote more definitively:

The sealing of the Spirit is no especial act but only an especial effect of his communication unto us. The effects of this sealing are gracious operations of the

---

37. Eph. 1:13; 4:30; 2 Cor. 1:22. I have given a more extensive review of this question in *John Owen on the Christian Life*, pp. 116–24.

38. *Works* 2:242.

39. "A Discourse on the Holy Spirit as a Comforter," in *Works* 4:351–419. It was published in 1693, ten years after his death.

COMMUNION WITH THE HOLY SPIRIT

Holy Spirit in and upon believers but the sealing itself
is the communication of the Spirit unto them.[40]

Perhaps conscious of the discussions that had taken place
among members of the Puritan Brotherhood, including his
own friends, Owen goes on to note:

It hath been generally conceived that this sealing of
the Spirit is that which gives assurance unto believers
and so indeed it doth, although the way whereby it
doth hath not been rightly apprehended. And therefore none has been able to declare the especial nature
of that act of the Spirit whereby he seals us when such
assurance should ensue. But it is indeed not any act of
the Spirit in us that is the ground of our assurance but
the communication of the Spirit to us.[41]

It is the Spirit Himself who is the seal. This brings Owen
back to our starting point: the Lord Jesus Christ is the One
whom the Father sealed.[42] He communicated the Spirit to
Him. What was true of Christ then becomes true for those
who are in Christ now. As the Spirit ministers as that seal,
assurance of grace and salvation follow.

Thus, the testimony of the Spirit that we are God's children

---

40. *Works* 4:404.
41. *Works* 4:405.
42. John 6:27.

117

is the effect of the presence of the seal of the Spirit, which activates the believer's sense of assurance. Owen provides a vivid word picture of this. The Christian, he says, by the power of his own conscience is brought before the law of God. There, the plea of the Christian's conscience is that he is a child of God. He "produceth all his evidences; everything whereby faith gives him an interest in God." There are reasons why he believes himself to be a true Christian. But, says Owen,

> Satan, in the meantime, opposeth with all his might; sin and law assist him; many flaws are found in his evidences; the truth of them all is questioned; and the soul hangs in suspense as to the issue. In the midst of the plea and contest the Comforter comes, and by a word of promise or otherwise overpowers the heart with a comfortable persuasion (and bears down all objections) that his plea is good and that he is a child of God. . . . When our spirits are pleading their right and title, he comes in and bears witness on our side.
>
> When the Lord Jesus at one word stilled the raging of the sea and wind, all that were with him knew that there was Divine power at hand, Matt. viii. 25–27. And when the Holy Ghost by one word stills the tumults and the storms that are raised in the soul, giving it an immediate calm and security, the soul knows his divine power, and rejoices in his presence.[43]

---

43. *Works* 2:241–42.

In a word, Owen is saying that the Spirit does in us as seal what Christ did for the disciples as Savior.

The reappearance of Matthew 8:25–27 here is, surely, significant. This, as we have seen, was Owen's "life verse," the text that, on that never-to-be-forgotten day in Aldermanbury Chapel, had brought him into the full light of assurance and joy in Christ. What we have here, in all probability, is a transcript of Owen's own experience, and the reason why communion with the Spirit was so significant to him.

Christ did not leave the Apostles as orphans,[44] nor does He leave us bereft of comforts. We receive blessings beyond our expectations. We are given the Spirit in order to live in prayerful communion with Him as He leads us into the enjoyment of all the blessings of our inheritance. And, Owen says by way of summary:

> These are,—his bringing the promises of Christ to remembrance, glorifying him in our hearts, shedding abroad the love of God in us, witnessing with us as to our spiritual estate and condition, sealing us to the day of redemption (being the earnest of our inheritance), anointing us with privileges as to their consolation, confirming our adoption, and being present with us in our supplications. Here is the wisdom of faith,— to find out and meet with the Comforter in all these things; not to lose their sweetness, by lying in the dark

---

44. John 14:18.

[as] to their author, nor coming short of the returns which are required of us.[45]

Such communion with the Spirit brings us consolation in afflictions, a peace that flows from the assurance that we are accepted before God, a joy that is ours as we share the anointing of the One who received the oil of gladness without limit, and a hope which brings stability and direction to our lives.

But what of the "returns" on our part of which Owen had spoken? What does all this mean for us in terms of our response to the privileges of communion with God?

OUR RETURNS

Three negative and three positive responses may be mentioned here. Before listing these, however, it is worthwhile to stand back and reflect on the structure of Owen's thinking. For the substance of what he writes makes such demands on his readers that it is easy to be so caught up in following it that we miss seeing its underlying structures. But the very fact that he thinks of the Christian's response ("returns") in both negative and positive terms is important.

The Spirit brings us into union with the *crucified* and *resurrected* Savior and therefore into communion with Him in His death and resurrection. Since this is, as it were, the ground on which the Spirit operates, it also becomes the pattern of the

---

45. *Works* 2:249.

Christian life: death and resurrection, mortification and viv-
ification, putting off the old and putting on the new. Gospel
negatives and gospel positives thus become the *leitmotif*, the
melody line, for all of our fellowship with the Son. This was
the Apostolic pattern.[46]

This, then, is why Owen gives us these three negative and
three positive exhortations.

Do Not Grieve the Spirit

The metaphor[47] (associated with Paul's words in Ephesians
4:30) is actually drawn from Isaiah's exposition of Israel's
post-exodus wilderness wanderings: "They rebelled and
grieved his Holy Spirit."[48] The Christian has entered into a
deeper and more intimate relationship with the Spirit and
must learn to be sensitive to His love, kindness, and tenderness. Even if the Spirit cannot be "passively grieved,"[49] we can
live in a way that is grievous to Him. He will respond to us *as
though He had been grieved* since we have become insensitive
to the offensiveness to Him of our spiritual indifference and
carelessness. The result is that "We lose both *the power and
pleasure* of our obedience."[50]

---

46. See, *inter alia*, Romans 13:11–14 and its fuller exposition in Colossians 3:1–17.

47. Owen's exposition suggests he sees this language as metaphorical or, in theological
terms, as an anthropopathism (describing God in terms of the emotional-affective
experience of humans). See *Works* 2:265.

48. Isa. 63:10.

49. *Works* 2:265.

50. *Works* 2:266. Italics original.

Owen heaps on our consciences motives for not grieving Him, and indicates what *positively* the believer is to do:

Let the soul, in the whole course of its obedience, exercise itself by faith to thoughts hereof, and lay due weight upon it: "The Holy Ghost, in his infinite love and kindness towards me, hath condescended to be my comforter; he doth it willingly, freely, powerfully. What have I received from him! In the multitude of my perplexities how hath he refreshed my soul! Can I live one day without his consolations? And shall I be regardless of him in that wherein he is concerned? Shall I grieve him by negligence, sin, and folly? Shall not his love constrain me to walk before him to all well pleasing?"[51]

Do Not Quench the Spirit

If the metaphor of "grieving" reflects on our *relationship* with the Spirit, "quenching" reflects on His *ministry*. The word picture that comes to Owen's mind is that of "wet wood . . . cast into the fire"[52]—a spirit and lifestyle that in effect hinder the gracious work of the Spirit as, like a fire, He burns in love for us and seeks to stir up a love for holiness within us. Rather than dampen inner promptings to faithfulness and obedience, we must learn to fan them into flame.

---

51. Ibid.
52. Ibid.

Do Not Resist His Word

Owen emphasizes the relationship between the Spirit and the Word—in this context from the ministry of Stephen. His opponents "could not withstand the wisdom and the Spirit with which he was speaking"[53]; they "always resist the Holy Spirit"[54] by resisting the prophetic word of God.

Here again, Owen is concerned about our spiritual vision and what we "eye" when we listen to the exposition of the Word. Fail to "eye" the ministry of the Spirit as He gives gifts to the church for her upbuilding—that is to say, see only mere men, no better and perhaps no more able than ourselves— and we inevitably reduce the preaching of God's Word to the words of men. It is then that we are in danger of belittling the Word, then resisting it, and ultimately despising it. Our calling, then, is to fix our gaze where it properly belongs: the Word is the Spirit's sword; its exposition is the Spirit's instrument to release the Word into our lives to do its work of conversion and transformation.

But as we do so, Owen urges us to remember that the Holy Spirit is the third person of the Divine Being, the One who proceeds from the Father and the Son, the eternal Spirit. He is therefore to be worshiped, loved, and adored. It is the ever-increasing Christlikeness to which this leads that is both the fruit of our communion with the Spirit and the goal in His communion with us.

---

53. Acts 6:10.
54. Acts 7:51.

Owen well understood that the Holy Spirit does not bring glory to Himself but to the Son. But this should not be used as an argument for our failing to give glory to the Spirit as well as to the Son and the Father. The role of the Spirit within the Trinitarian economy does not minimize His full deity, nor does it exempt us from worshiping Him. Rather, the Spirit's role calls forth from our hearts admiration, adoration, praise, and devotion to the One who so lovingly shines on the Son and comes to us as the Spirit of grace. Because this is His ministry, we have all the more reason to worship the Spirit together with the Father and the Son.

Here, if anywhere, the comment—albeit intended in another sense altogether—is actually true: the Holy Spirit has been the "forgotten person" of the Godhead. Perhaps, then, as we hear it across the centuries, John Owen's voice will help awaken us to the ways in which we may have grieved, quenched, and resisted the Holy Spirit.

Praise Father, Son, and Holy Ghost

For luminous exposition, and powerful defence of Scriptural doctrine—for determined enforcement of practical obligation—for skillful anatomy of the self-deceitfulness of the heart—and for a detailed and wise treatment of the diversified exercises of the Christian's heart, he [John Owen] stands probably unrivaled.[1]

—CHARLES BRIDGES

Our "chief end," according to the Westminster Shorter Catechism, is "to glorify God and to enjoy him forever."[2] Glorifying God means worshiping Him as God, for "the *divine nature* is the reason and cause of all worship."[3] Consequently, "it is impossible to *worship any* one person, and not worship

---

1. Charles Bridges, *The Christian Ministry*, 6th ed. (London: Seeley, Burnside, and Seeley, 1844), p. 41.

2. WSC 1.

3. *Works* 2:268. Italics original.

the whole Trinity."[4] This principle brings Owen full circle in his theology.

In God's activity within His three-personal being, all three persons are always involved and engaged (*opera Trinitatis ad intra sunt indivisa*). So too, His activity in relation to the created order is always the work of all three persons (*opera Trinitatis ad extra sunt indivisa*), even when one person exercises a particular function (appropriations).

Owen is at one here with the fathers of the church, who developed the doctrine known as *perichōrēsis* or *circumincessio*[5] —that in everything God the Trinity is and does, each of the three persons relates to and engages with each of the other persons. The "choreography" of the Divine Being is beautifully one in its diversity and diverse in its unity. Both internally and externally, the persons of the Trinity always function in the harmony of a single Deity. We therefore never worship any person as though His personhood could be in any way abstracted or separated from His participation in the single essence of His deity.

This, of course, is the mystery of the Trinity, into which the human mind can never fully penetrate. Yet this is not only

---

4. Ibid. Italics original.

5. This reality is clearly present in the New Testament, in which a specific action is attributed to Father or Son or Holy Spirit, yet almost always within the context of reference being made to one or both of the other persons. As a theological construct, it is present already in Origen's exposition of the "special working" (the Father) or "special ministry" (the Son) or "grace" (the Spirit) of each person. See Origen's *De Principiis*, 1.3.7–8, in which he appeals to 1 Corinthians 12:4–6 for the principle.

because our minds are fallen, and therefore both darkened and twisted. For before the thrice-holy One, even seraphim who have never sinned veil their faces and cover their feet. Here, members of the family of God in both its heavenly and earthly branches can only gaze from the shoreline on the crystal sea on which is reflected the eternal majesty and glory of the triune God, "lost in wonder, love, and praise."

It is into this life of fellowship with God that we were baptized—into the grace of the Lord Jesus, the love of the heavenly Father, and the communion of the Holy Spirit. And, of course, it is at the Lord's Supper that we taste and enjoy this life in its simplest expression. For here, we are invited by Christ Himself to taste and see that He is good, and to feed on Him. As we do so, the Spirit engages in the work He loves, the work of taking what belongs to Christ and making it known to us. As Horatius Bonar, who stood in the Owenian tradition two centuries removed, would express it:

> Here, O my Lord, I see thee face to face;
> Here would I touch and handle things unseen;
> Here grasp with firmer faith the eternal grace,
> And all my weariness upon thee lean.[6]

And, as through the Spirit we enjoy fellowship with the Son, we remember that "God [the Father] so loved the world,

---

6. From the hymn "Here O My Lord I See Thee Face to Face" by Horatius Bonar (1808–89).

that he gave his only Son, that whoever believes in him should not perish but have eternal life."[7] We are drawn into the love of God and anticipate the day when the Marriage Supper He has prepared for His Son will take place.

Just as we have been baptized into the name of the Trinity, we enjoy fellowship with each person in His distinctive expressions of grace toward us. As we do so, the frequently sung words of the "Doxology," now better understood, give expression to our affections. For we have been loved by the Father, reconciled through the Son, and are being transformed "from one degree of glory to another" by the Spirit. Thus, we sing:

> Praise God, from whom all blessings flow;
> Praise him, all creatures here below;
> Praise him above, ye heavenly host:
> Praise Father, Son, and Holy Ghost.[8]

Well might we say in response: "Amen, and amen!"

---

7. John 3:16.
8. The final verse of the hymns "Awake, My Soul, and with the Sun" and "Glory to Thee, My God, This Night," written by Thomas Ken (1637–1711), himself a student at Oxford toward the end of Owen's administration as vice-chancellor.

BIBLIOGRAPHY

Barth, Karl. *The Word of God and the Word of Man.* Translated by D. Horton. New York: Harper and Row, 1957.

Bellarmine, Robert. *De Justificatione.* In *Disputationes de Controversiis Christianae Fidei adversus huius Temporaris Haerticos.* 4 vols. Cologne, Germany: B. Gualterhus, 1619.

Bridges, Charles. *The Christian Ministry.* 6th ed. London: Seeley, Burnside, and Seeley, 1844.

Calvin, John. *Commentary on 2 Corinthians, 1 and 2 Timothy, Titus, Philemon.* Edited by D.W. and T.F. Torrance. Translated by T.A. Smail. Edinburgh, Scotland: Oliver and Boyd, 1964.

Chalmers, Thomas. *Select Works of Thomas Chalmers.* Vol. 1. Minneapolis: Robert Carter, 1848.

Cotton, John. *A Commentary Upon the First Epistle General of John.* London: Thomas Parkhurst, 1658.

Durham, James. *Song of Solomon.* Reprint, Edinburgh, Scotland: Banner of Truth Trust, 1997.

Ferguson, Sinclair B. *The Holy Spirit.* Downers Grove, Ill.: InterVarsity Press, 1996.

———. *John Owen on the Christian Life*. Edinburgh, Scotland: Banner of Truth, 1987.

———. Introduction to *The Priesthood of Christ, Its Necessity and Nature*, by John Owen. Fearn, Ross-shire, Scotland: Christian Focus, 2010.

Fraser, Antonia. *Cromwell, Our Chief of Men*. London: Weidenfeld and Nicolson, 1975.

Goodwin, Thomas. *Of the Object and Acts of Justifying Faith.* In *The Works of Thomas Goodwin*. Edited by Thomas Smith. Edinburgh, Scotland: James Nichol, 1864.

Griffiths, Stephen M. *Redeem the Time: The Problem of Sin in the Writings of John Owen.* Fearn, Ross-shire, Scotland: Christian Focus, 2001.

Kant, Immanuel. *The Conflict of the Faculties.* Translated by Mary J. Gregor. New York: Abaris Books, 1979.

Kenyon, J.P. *Stuart England.* 2nd ed. London: Penguin Books, 1985.

Matthews, A.G. Introduction to *The Savoy Declaration of Faith and Order 1658*, p. 12. Edited by A.G. Matthews. London: Independent Press, 1959.

Nietzsche, Friedrich. *Thus Spake Zarathustra.* Edited by Adrian Del Caro and Robert Pippin. Cambridge Texts in the History of Philosophy. Cambridge, England: Cambridge University Press, 2006.

Orme, William. *Memoirs of the Life, Writings, and Religious Connexions of John Owen, D.D.* London, 1810.

Owen, John. *The Correspondence of John Owen (1616-1683): With an Account of His Life and Work.* Edited by Peter Toon. Cambridge, England: James Clarke, 1970.

———. *On Communion with God the Father, Son, and Holy Ghost, each person distinctly, in love, grace, and consolation; or, The Saints' Fellowship with the Father, Son, and Holy*

Ghost Unfolded. In vol. 2 of *The Works of John Owen*. Edited by W.H. Goold. Edinburgh, Scotland: Johnstone and Hunter, 1850–55. Reprint, London: Banner of Truth Trust, 1966.

———. *The Oxford Orations of Dr. John Owen*. Edited by Peter Toon. Callington, Cornwall, England: Gospel Communication, 1971.

———. *The Works of John Owen*. Edited by Thomas Russell. 21 vols. London: Robert Baynes, 1826.

———. *The Works of John Owen*. Edited by W.H. Goold. 24 vols. Edinburgh, Scotland: Johnstone and Hunter, 1850–55. Reprint, London: Banner of Truth Trust, 1966.

Ryken, Leland. *Worldly Saints*. Grand Rapids, Mich.: Zondervan, 1986.

Ryle, J.C. *Holiness: Its Nature, Hindrances, Difficulties, and Roots*. Cambridge, England: James Clarke, 1952.

Selderhuis, H.J., ed. *The Calvin Handbook*. Grand Rapids, Mich.: Eerdmans, 2009.

Spurgeon, Charles Haddon. *Commenting and Commentaries*. London: Passmore and Alabaster, 1876.

Thomson, Andrew. *Life of Dr Owen*. In vol. 1 of *The Works of John Owen*. Edited by W.H. Goold. Edinburgh, Scotland: Johnstone and Hunter, 1850–55. Reprint, London: Banner of Truth Trust, 1966.

Toon, Peter. *God's Statesman: The Life and Work of John Owen, Pastor, Educator, Theologian*. Exeter, England: Paternoster Press, 1971.

Trueman, Carl R. *John Owen: Reformed Catholic, Renaissance Man*. Farnham, Surrey, England: Ashgate, 2007.

Turretin, Francis. *Institutes of Elenctic Theology*. Translated by George M. Giger. Edited by James T. Dennison Jr. 3 vols. Phillipsburg, N.J.: Presbyterian and Reformed, 1992.

Vindication of Owen by a Friendly Scrutiny. Cited by Andrew Thomson, *Life of Dr Owen*. In vol. 1 of *The Works of John Owen*. Edited by W.H. Goold. Edinburgh, Scotland: Johnstone and Hunter, 1850–55. Reprint, London: Banner of Truth Trust, 1966..

Warfield, B.B. *Calvin as a Theologian and Calvinism Today*. Philadelphia: Presbyterian Board of Publication, 1909. Reprint, London: Evangelical Press, n.d.

Wood, Anthony. *Athenae Oxoniensis*. London, 1691. 3rd ed. Edited by Philip Bliss. London, 1813–20. Cited by Andrew Thomson, *Life of Dr Owen*. In vol. 1 of *The Works of John Owen*. Edited by W.H. Goold. Edinburgh, Scotland: Johnstone and Hunter, 1850–55. Reprint, London: Banner of Truth Trust, 1966.

SCRIPTURE INDEX

SUBJECT INDEX

ABOUT THE AUTHOR

Dr. Sinclair B. Ferguson is a Ligonier Ministries teaching fellow, Chancellor's Professor of Systematic Theology at Reformed Theological Seminary, and the evening preacher at St. Peter's Free Church in Dundee, Scotland. He previously served as senior minister of the historic First Presbyterian Church in Columbia, S.C.

A graduate of the University of Aberdeen, Scotland, Dr. Ferguson is author of some fifty books, including *The Whole Christ*, *Devoted to God*, *In Christ Alone: Living the Gospel-Centered Life*, *The Holy Spirit*, *Grow in Grace*, *Let's Study Philippians*, and *Some Pastors and Teachers*. His writing interests have ranged from scholarly works to books for children.

He has served as minister of two congregations in Scotland, one on Unst, the most northerly inhabited island in the United Kingdom, and the other in the center of Glasgow, the largest city in Scotland.